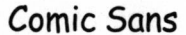

Comic Sans

Also by Simon Garfield:

Expensive Habits
The End of Innocence
The Wrestling
The Nation's Favourite
Mauve
The Last Journey of William Huskisson
Our Hidden Lives (ed.)
We Are at War (ed.)
Private Battles (ed.)
The Error World
Mini
Exposure
Just My Type
On the Map
To the Letter
My Dear Bessie (ed.)
A Notable Woman (ed.)
Timekeepers
In Miniature
Dog's Best Friend
All the Knowledge in the World
Albertus
Baskerville

Comic Sans

* * *

The Biography of a Typeface

Simon Garfield

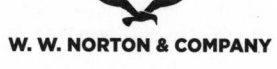

W. W. NORTON & COMPANY

Independent Publishers Since 1923

For information about permission to reproduce selections from this book,
write to Permissions, W. W. Norton & Company, Inc.,
500 Fifth Avenue, New York, NY 10110

For information about special discounts for bulk purchases,
please contact W. W. Norton Special Sales at
specialsales@wwnorton.com or 800-233-4830

Manufacturing by Versa Press

ISBN 978-1-324-08624-6

W. W. Norton & Company, Inc.
500 Fifth Avenue, New York, N.Y. 10110
www.wwnorton.com

W. W. Norton & Company Ltd.
15 Carlisle Street, London W1D 3BS

1 2 3 4 5 6 7 8 9 0

Contents

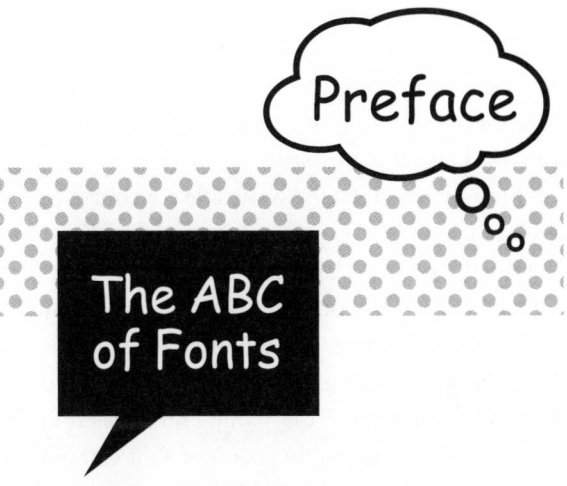

Preface

The ABC of Fonts

The moving walkway from Venice airport to your water taxi will take eight minutes with a heavy case if you really get a move on.

The sign announcing this is in a type often used for signage – probably Univers or Transport or Frutiger, or one of those. It appears several times on your journey – eight minutes, six minutes, two minutes. On your metallic way you can either look at the car park and other concrete things beyond the window, or the illuminated adverts for Cartier, Brioni and Bulgari, all of which have a luxurious type we might associate with glamour and eye-watering prices. This typeface will often be something French like Optima, Berton Sans or Maquna, or one of those. Thin and thick highly tapered strokes, a bit of furl and curl, often an elegant calligraphic hand suggesting a signature or a thank you note dashed off with haste.

But then you're at the waterside concourse with a choice. The open-top private water taxi to the grand canal will cost €130 and will remind you of a film with Dirk Bogarde or Julie Christie, but the water bus is only €26 return, and although it will make you feel cramped and a bit stuffy, it's how the locals do it. This is the Alilaguna, the name emblazoned on its side in a badly modified version of Comic Sans, or Chalkboard SE, or one of those, friendly and amateur, trying hard to say 'welcome aboard!', even on the murkiest February afternoon.

It's a forty-minute trip. I suggest getting on the blue line (rather than red) and asking for Fondamente Nove, the second stop. You're on solid land now. From here it's a couple of bridges and a couple of cafés before you turn right into Calle del Fumo, a long narrow alley, and about thirty metres in you'll get to a printer named Gianni Basso.

This, in essence, is where commercial printing begins. In the early 1470s, Nicolas Jenson and Johannes de Colonia brought everything they had learnt about moveable metal type from Gutenberg in Germany, and everything they had liked in the new letter forms used by the printers Pannartz and Sweynheym at Subiaco on the outskirts of Rome, and set themselves up to print half of Venice's books. They were joined by Aldus Manutius and his letter cutter Francisco Griffo, who would popularise italics and the concept of the smaller portable book, and they would be in competition with Franciscus Renner, Bernardinus Stagninus, Johannes and Vindelinus da Spira, Florentius de Argentina, Gabriele and Filippo di Pietro, among many others. Together, before 1500, they would print more books in this tiny cosmopolitan city than anywhere else in Europe, slightly more than Paris and Rome, vastly more than London.*

At the age of sixty-nine, Gianni Basso is the most famous printer in town, although these days it's mostly business cards and other stationery. He has thick grey hair with a proper parting, a generous paunch and an enthusiastic manner. He is everyone's pal, and his vanity compels him to remove his glasses for a photograph. His printing office has several letterpress machines, greased and inked and clanking

---

* See the Incunabula Short Title Catalogue at the British Library, a listing of more than 30,000 editions. The Venetian printers account for more than a tenth of the total (some 3835 titles). Printing in London, William Caxton accounts for a mere 125.

away, a couple of them automatic and the others hand-fed, the majority from early in the last century with worn nameplates from Milan and Turin. He's been here for forty years, and he's had a celebrity client for each of them: the Sultan of Brunei, Lord Euston, Nigella Lawson, people from Apple wanting something old and original, people from Buckingham Palace with orders to accompany their Canaletto show. There's no email for him, and no sign of a computer, but a visit or the post will secure an order for letterheads in the type of your choice, Garamond, Bodoni, Italia and Augustea always popular, all on that lovely smooth wove paper which may transport you to a drawing room in Georgian England, the steep prices reflecting the fine quality.

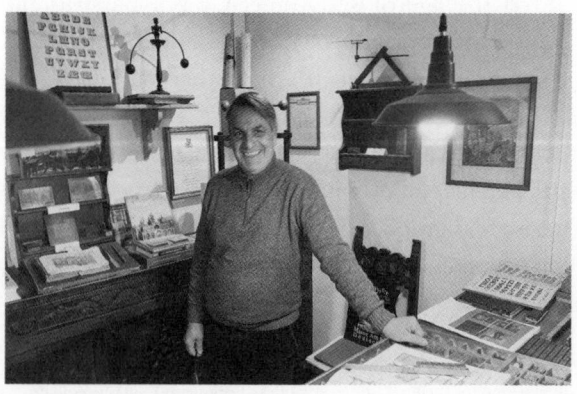

Upholding the grand tradition: the Gutenberg of Venice in his printshop.

He used to offer Baskerville in many sizes too, but the letters, stored in cases close to the floor, were ruined after the last big *aqua alta* flood in 2019, and he's yet to find a set to replace them.

There are many modern types to be found all over Venice. The elaborate hand-painted signs above the old *gelaterie* are particularly attractive, as lush and swirly as their product, today reflected in modern fonts such as Budge, Gelato Script and Salsero. At the Biennale there's always plenty of Helvetica Neue, Futura, Favourit and Verlag. In the Rialto, the Fondaco dei Tedeschi, once the central post office, is now a glamorous department store; the Amo restaurant in the atrium offers lots of things with truffles, with branding all in Albertus.

But there are few modern types to be found in Gianni Basso's print shop. Orders reach him from all over the world addressed to 'Gutenberg of Venice', which he, of course, encourages. Basso likes anything that associates him with the mucky glories of old metal letters and inked wood poster types, and his walls are covered in newspaper cuttings marvelling at these revels. Opposite his office is a shop selling funeral ornaments, pots for a loved-one's ashes and the like. One of his two sons may be interested in taking over the business when he dies, although he is also interested in skiing. Basso

is encouraged and always surprised that young
people are intrigued by 'the museum' that he runs
next to his print shop. Here is the old lead and
wooden type and the cases and all the necessary
tools for traditional printing, and here are the old
typeface sample books from long-disbanded printing foundries in Italy and France. There are a lot of
books explaining both theory and technique, among
them the thoughts of Bruce Rogers ('One can take
almost any kind of type & produce extremely varied
results by different methods of handling it…') and
Stanley Morison ('Even dullness and monotony in
the typesetting are far less vicious to a reader than
typographical eccentricity…').

When I visited in February 2023, I fell once more
for the romance of this world. With this machinery
my great-grandparents got on in business; this is
how all my distant family studied their professions,
dentists and motherhood and the law, and this is
how I learnt to read. I am fond of the concept of
the moon missions being only made possible by
people navigating in canoes many centuries before,
and so it is here. This is why people from Apple and
Google come here and drool a little, for this is what
they couldn't cancel. The digital takeover, slow and
benign at first, and then overwhelming and fatal,
has not entirely obliterated the human desire to

see words reproduced in the old way. We forget this early craft – this distant echo of Nicolas Jenson and his friends – at our great loss.

In 2004, following the results of a survey that noted a decline in 'reading for pleasure', Andrew Solomon lamented the potential impact of this trend. 'The metaphoric quality of writing,' he wrote in the *New York Times*, '– the fact that so much can be expressed through the rearrangement of 26 shapes on a piece of paper – is as exciting as the idea of a complete genetic code made up of four bases: man's work on a par with nature's. Discerning the patterns of those arrangements is the essence of civilization.'

Solomon's observation resonates. For this is what this book is about, the formation of letters as the cornerstone of progress, diversity and ambition. The book forms part of a series (the others examine Albertus and Baskerville), each designed to show how one typeface came into being and then transformed the landscape. It will examine how a font does not magically appear, but is a result of intention and historical progression, and often an attempt to solve a problem (usually the problem is 'how do I make these words clear, convincing and appealing?'). It will show that the application of a font varies over time and will fade in and out of fashion, and it will ask why a few typefaces endure while most leave barely a trace.*

Technological advance has not spoiled the letterform, even as it pixelates it. In fact the opposite is true: the proliferation of computers and word processing has made us all lords of type, the pull-down menu a modern plaything. Even the Kindle offers a choice of the established faces Baskerville, Futura, Palatino and Helvetica, alongside the new proprietary styles Bookerly and Amazon Ember. This little book will explain where another of these drop-down options comes from.

After I'd made an order for some letter paper, Basso handed me a gift, a print, carefully laid on thick copper-coloured paper, of a poem he has hanging in both shop and museum: Beatrice Warde's 1932 broadside *This Is A Printing Office*. This is a sign (a proclamation, a hope, a protest, never actually intended as a poem but as lyrical as Milton) that was once displayed in every old-fashioned hot-metal workroom with a sense of its own worth. Basso's version was in Garamond, but here it is in Comic Sans Bold, something you're unlikely to see too often.

---

* I am using the words typeface and font interchangeably here, as is the colloquial way. Strictly, a typeface is the big, overall name for a design (Baskerville), while font denotes a particular style or weight within a typeface family (Baskerville Bold, or Baskerville Italic).

THIS IS A

PRINTING OFFICE

*

CROSSROADS OF CIVILISATION

REFUGE OF ALL THE ARTS

AGAINST THE RAVAGES OF TIME

ARMOURY OF FEARLESS TRUTH

AGAINST WHISPERING RUMOUR

INCESSANT TRUMPET OF TRADE

*

FROM THIS PLACE **WORDS** MAY FLY ABROAD

NOT TO PERISH ON WAVES OF SOUND
NOT TO VARY WITH THE WRITER'S HAND
BUT FIXED IN TIME
HAVING BEEN VERIFIED BY PROOF

*

FRIEND, YOU STAND ON SACRED GROUND
THIS IS A PRINTING OFFICE

You may assume that because this book concerns itself primarily with Comic Sans, it will necessarily contain jokes, or at the very least irony. I can't really comment on that, except to say that when I told people I was writing it they tended to wrinkle their nose.

Like the old wrestler Mick McManus, Comic Sans is the one that Everyone Loves To Hate. Personally, I love to love it, and I hope, after reading this, you will too. More than anything, I hope you will love the *idea* of Comic Sans, the concept of a set of letters that got people who aren't really interested in type of any kind suddenly intrigued, and sometimes cross. Type is about opinion, about the choices one makes to present something for reading. Do we want it to stand out or do we want it to blend in and go unnoticed? Do we want formality or a casual feel? Do we want to sell something, and thereby associate a typeface with something we have bought beneficially before? If you're a fan of Colleen Hoover, and frankly I am yet to meet anyone who is (despite the fact that she is currently the bestselling author in the world), then you might be susceptible to a book designed with a similar typeface to the tough blocky one used on Colleen's paperbacks, a combination of Din Condensed Variable and Gambler Gothic Regular, which to my eyes is a far more objectionable face than Comic Sans. Still, enough of Colleen. For now.

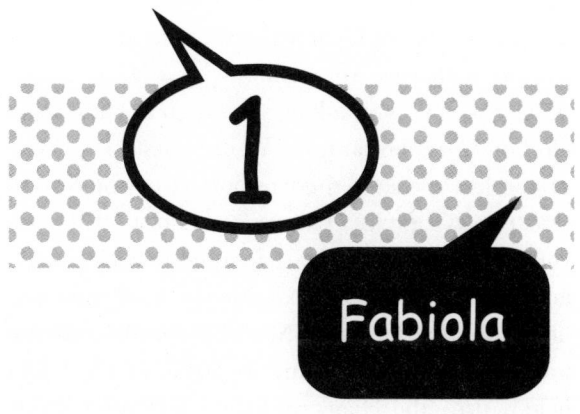

1

Fabiola

On the morning of 4 July 2012 there was big news from CERN, the European Organization for Nuclear Research in Geneva. The Italian physicist Fabiola Gianotti spoke of her immense honour to be announcing, after a forty-year search, a subatomic particle with the expected properties of a Higgs boson. Gianotti was presenting the results of ATLAS, one of the two experiments within the Large Hadron Collider that lay at the heart of the discovery. She addressed a vast assembly of media with a mixture of pride, good humour and extreme exhaustion.

Many of the journalists, recognising that this was a breakthrough of immense proportions, but not knowing quite why, asked for an explanation 'in lay terms'. One of Gianotti's colleagues told them it was 'clear that we are dealing with a Higgs boson, though we still have a long way to go to know what kind of Higgs boson it is'. Well thanks a lot. Some of the less specialised correspondents would soon resort to Wikipedia. The excitement at CERN revolved around evidence that some particles could acquire mass, 'and the exposure of an elementary particle in the Standard Model of particle physics produced by the quantum excitation of the Higgs field'. Also, 'the Higgs particle is a massive scalar boson with zero spin'. Everyone in the room made notes and checked their recording equipment, and editors were informed that this was finally it, at last.

After the initial announcement, Fabiola Gianotti took to her slideshow. This too was a chewy proposition. Her deck emphasised that the results were preliminary. She explained that the experimental conditions were 'harsher' in 2012 due to a 'x2 larger event pile-up'. In the high-mass resolution 'the pile-up was robust'. Her next slide showed peak luminosity. She ended her presentation with a photo of a crowd of people gathered around a circular desk of computer screens, and they were all clapping and smiling. This was a section of her team, and the text on the slide read:

BIG THANKS

To the whole LHC exploitation team,

including the operation, technical

and infrastructure groups, for the

OUTSTANDING performances

of the machine, and to all the

people who have contributed to the

conception, design, construction and

operation of this superb instrument.

Almost immediately there were two headlines, two Higgs boson stories running concurrently. The first – in almost every print and online newspaper in the world – was news of the Higgs boson. The second, across many design-based online sites, and almost all of Twitter, was the news that the announcement of the Higgs boson had been delivered in Comic Sans. Not just the thank-you to her team, but all the results in all their complexity. Hilarity competed with outrage: this huge scientific breakthrough, perhaps the greatest of the internet age, had been presented to a live worldwide audience in a Microsoft font that had few competitors when it came to universal derision. Even those with the most rudimentary experience of PowerPoint knew that you didn't present with this typeface. Comic Sans was an alphabet for children, for children's party invitations with a promise of fun and games. It was not, and never would be, the

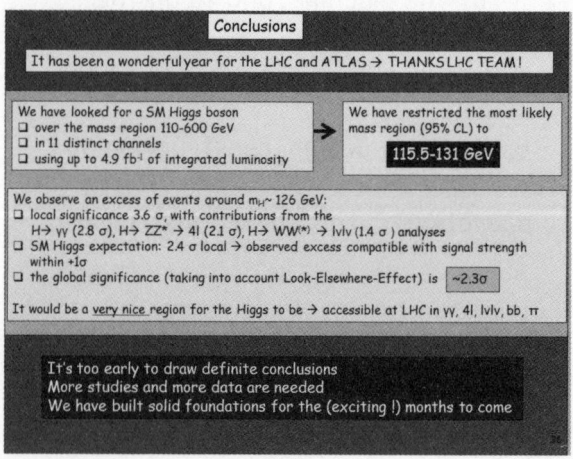

And in conclusion … Exciting results presented in an unexpected way.

choice for announcing significant developments in particle mass, much less any aspect of quantum field theory.

So what happened? Rolf Heuer, CERN's director-general, opened the press conference with the news that he and his colleagues had endured many sleepless nights in the run-up to their announcement. Could it be that, in formulating her slide deck, Fabiola Gianotti – the woman who would succeed Heuer as director-general, the first female in that role – was simply too tired or too incautious to care about typeface choice?

Lisa Randall, the first tenured female professor of theoretical physics at Harvard, was wondering the same thing, and emailed Gianotti with congratulations and the big question. Why Comic Sans?

'Because I like it,' Gianotti replied.

> You Don't Clown Around with a Clown

2

Because this story is about Comic Sans, the most disagreed-upon and tweeted-about assemblage of letters in the history of the world, a consideration which includes Times New Roman and Helvetica, not to mention the original dark Germanic type favoured by Johannes Gutenberg, the CERN story has its inevitable echoes.

The year after the Higgs boson discovery, Dr Peter Higgs, then aged eighty-four, of the University of Edinburgh, and Dr François Englert, then eighty, of the Université Libre de Bruxelles, were awarded the Nobel Prize in Physics for their work enhancing our understanding of the origin of mass of subatomic particles. 'I am overwhelmed to receive this award and thank the Royal Swedish Academy,' Higgs said in a statement. Englert said, 'You may imagine that this is not very unpleasant.'

This news, and these quotes, now appears on the Nobel Prize website in a typeface named Alfred Regular, or Alfred Sans, designed in 2018 to unify the Nobel brand (previously each department had its own look). It was made by Stockholm Design Lab, who were also responsible for logo and brand rethinks for Ericsson, Adidas and IKEA, and was inspired by the unnamed font engraved on the Nobel gold medal from 1902. There were also serif versions for text and display, each with an italic. It is a gentle, accessible and versatile type with a geometric preference and a suggestion of art nouveau, and was intended to reflect a timeless and universal impression of free-thinking and openness. Although Alfred Regular contains some proprietary twists, a very similar version named Ivar is available commercially in many sizes and weights from the digital foundry Letters from Sweden.

In early April 2014, two years after the Higgs boson announcement, and one year after the award of the Nobel prizes for the work, CERN unveiled a rebrand of its own, something to bring it further into the digital age. As was now commonplace, the new look would use its own typeface across all its sites, something easily translatable into all languages. The news was heralded by a brief YouTube video of Fabiola Gianotti (of course) announcing the switch: 'As of today, CERN web pages will be written in Comic Sans.' She was also quoted in the accompanying press release: 'When preparing my Higgs presentation, at first I had Georgia on my mind. But when I saw the closely spaced, slightly squishy rounded characters in my drop-down menu, I knew in my heart that Comic Sans was the right way to go.'

And there it was, the entire home page:

At CERN ... physicists and engineers are probing the fundamental structure of the universe

You may, by this point, have detected that something was up, and your suspicions would soon be confirmed. 'We wanted to make a bold visual statement,' said head of communications James Gillies. 'We thought the most effective way to communicate our research into the fundamental structure of matter at the very boundaries of technology was by changing the font.' And then the April Fool got sillier still: 'CERN management also decreed that especially important physics results would from now on be accompanied online by animations of little clappy hands.' The next day, a reset. The organisation got back to its exciting business in its traditional dull typefaces Droid Sans WRG Bold and Generous Sans Medium.

One reason that Comic Sans never works as an April Fool – and there have been several attempts before and since, including Google's announcement in 2011 that it would henceforth deliver all its search results in the font – is that you don't clown around with a clown. The giveaway can always be found in the announcement itself. 'Following some rigorous user testing of 41 different fonts,' it claimed, already over-egging it in tone and number, 'investigating how each affected user experience, we discovered one font consistently outperformed all others when it comes to user satisfaction, level of engagement, understanding web content, productivity, click-through rates and conversion rates: Comic Sans.'

Similarly, no one could ever believe that Comic Sans could be used, say, on the side of ambulances, or on gravestones, or to inscribe the winners on the metal plates of European football trophies. There are less characterful and colourful types for those kinds of duties. Times New Roman. Albertus. Baskerville. Even Georgia, even Verdana, still fresh and plain and new despite their age and ubiquity.

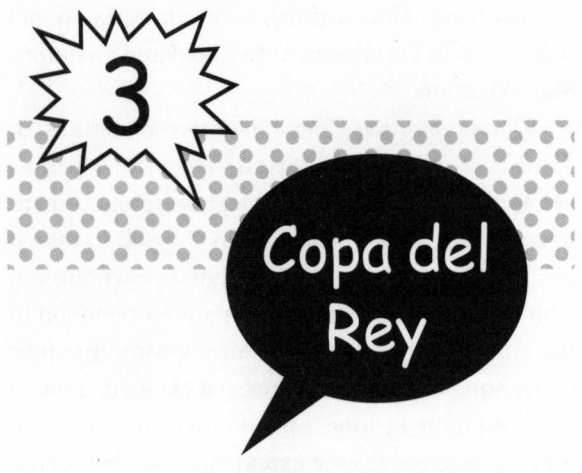

In late September 2022, an email from the graphic designer Paweł Adamek arrives at the podcast *Football Clichés*, an obsessive and entertaining listen from The Athletic about how we talk when we talk about the national game. The recipient is Adam Hurrey, the host; for this episode his guests are The Athletic journalists Charlie Eccleshare and Nick Miller:

> Hi Adam, I thought this could be of potential
> interest. I visited the Camp Nou recently [the
> home of Barcelona FC]. I couldn't help but notice
> that loads of the trophies in their trophy cabinet
> had their text engraved in the font of none other
> than Comic Sans, including the La Liga and Copa
> del Rey. [Adamek's former clients include the
> National Air and Space Museum in Washington
> DC, the Postal Museum in London and Marks
> & Spencer.] Which is insane, because it's a shit
> font and a bizarrely inappropriate choice for
> this purpose.

Hurrey asked Eccleshare how he felt about Comic Sans being used on such an important trophy, adding 'I wouldn't even accept it at Under-13s level'.

Eccleshare said he'd be so disappointed if he'd worked so hard for something and it was so devalued in that way.

Miller added that Comic Sans looked like a slightly trickier font to engrave than one of the more traditional ones.

Hurrey said that the designer of the font has had to defend it a lot. 'It's become infinitely shit, hasn't it, of course? Almost ironically so. He defended his font almost like Alex Ferguson defending his signing of Juan Sebastián Verón. He says, "If you love it, you don't know much about typography. But if you hate it, you really don't know much about typography either, and you should get another hobby."'

'That is punchy!' Charlie Eccleshare said.

'He went on to say that Comic Sans does what it was commissioned to do,' Hurrey continued. 'It's loved by kids, mums, dads and many family members. It did its job very well. It matched the brief.'

'I can see his frustration there,' Eccleshare added. He's like, "Obviously don't use it on the Copa del Rey. That's not on me. I designed it for kids."'

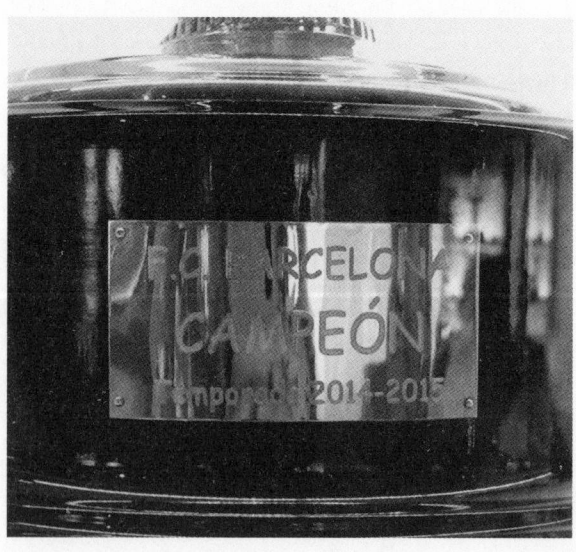

Messi type? Barcelona triumph again.

Hurrey then asked Nick Miller what font would look better on a trophy. 'Times New Roman would be fine, right?'

'Yeah probably,' Miller said. 'Helvetica? The design classic – that would look quite nice I think.'

As Hurrey later wrote in his column, the debate wasn't new. The anomaly of Comic Sans had been noted in 2010 by Spanish newspaper *La Vanguardia*, whose writer had pinned the blame, as he saw it, on a jeweller in Madrid named Fernando Alegre. The Copa del Rey had recently been won for the fifth time by Sevilla, enabling the club to keep the trophy for good. Señor Alegre was entrusted to make a new trophy, and select a typeface for its engraving. *La Vanguardia* did not ask him about his choice, but it did weigh in on its appropriateness. Comic Sans was not the ideal choice, being better suited for 'PowerPoint presentations made by school children, informal texts, and obnoxious email chains'.*

---

* When I emailed Hurrey about his podcast conversation, and whether he knew of any other instances where Comic Sans had been used on a major trophy, he replied that he knew of no others. He pointed me towards the controversy over the type used on the 2022 England football shirts, a nasty jagged affair on which players' names appeared in all upper case, apart from players with an i in their name (BELLiNGHAM; DiER) which appeared, quite inexplicably, in lower case.

These days, Hurrey noted, Comic Sans 'has been so historically ridiculed that it's actually become *uncool* to ridicule it'.

Did this, therefore, now make it cool?

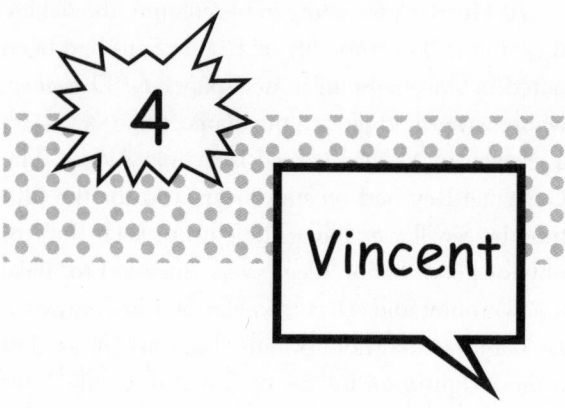

Vincent Connare became interested in type when he was eighteen. His main talent at high school in Milford, Massachusetts, was for baseball – he was a gifted outfielder – and he took up accountancy at university primarily because the baseball coach taught accounting. But then he hurt his arm and quit, and a job in a newspaper darkroom was followed by a job at Compugraphic, a company making the latest typesetting equipment. 'Before that I thought type was boring, just letters,' he told me. At home he used to copy the archaic German black-letter masthead of the *Boston Globe*, thinking nothing of its leaden connotations. 'But then I learnt that type was more than letters. It was whole stories and big business.'

His own early preference was for Courier, a typeface that most closely resembled letters on a typewriter. He would later set his resumé in Palatino, the humanist face modelled on the calligraphic broad-nibbed hand of the Renaissance (when he first sketched it in the mid-1940s, its designer Herman Zapf had called it Medici). The main reason Connare liked it was because his girlfriend used it for her college thesis.

Connare worked at Compugraphic from 1987 to 1993, the four-to-midnight shift, redrawing and converting existing typeface libraries to fit new software formats, using a program called Ikarus to modify the architecture of a font from phototypesetting to digital use. His clients included Hewlett Packard, Apple and others. One of the others was Microsoft, and after the successful completion of a project he was asked to join the company.

At Microsoft he was called a typographic engineer. 'It was nothing like traditional type production,' he remembers. 'It was me in a room not answering to anybody and not following the rules.

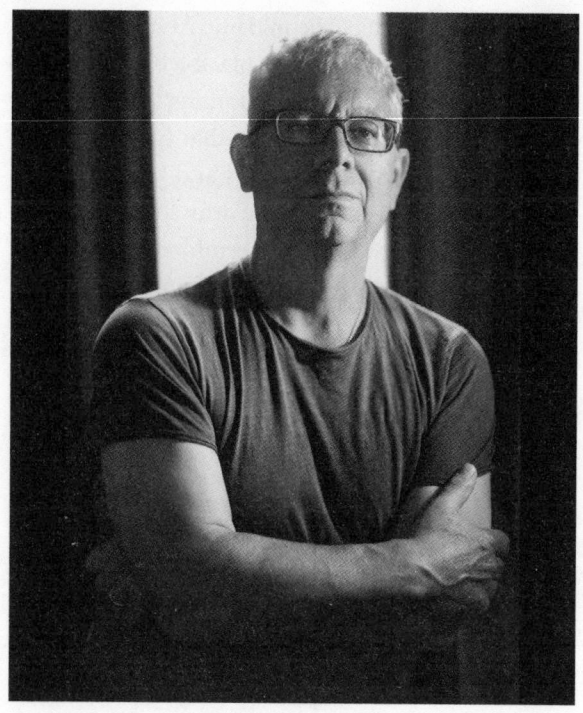

Not following the rules: 'typographic engineer' Vincent Connare.

In the nineties there was this punk mentality around digital type because it was still quite new – all kinds of wacky stuff – people were scanning things in and converting and stealing.'

In the mid-nineties, Microsoft was constantly re-structuring and reassessing its business. Based at the headquarters in Redmond, Washington, Connare was faced with new tasks every few months and found himself in a different building every year. 'We used to have a Tannoy system and somebody came in to say we should turn it off to improve efficiency. And it worked. I can only remember one message over the Tannoy – a message to locate Bill Gates for a TV interview. In my early days I shared an office with someone who only came in at lunchtime and worked with the lights off.'

In a group of around fifteen software programmers and testers, Connare became a fence between engineers and designers. 'They didn't think like each other. Someone would ask "can that flag we have be made to wave?" And the answer would be no. But actually the right answer would be "not yet", because a program didn't yet exist that would make it wave, so I would try to make that happen.

'For the first couple of years the type group was called the Windows Accessories Group, like we were making curtains.' Connare's time at Microsoft coincided with the huge increase in demand for personal computers, in turn resulting in a great scramble for typefaces for drop-down menus.

'Microsoft would take anything. As far as type went, you couldn't have enough.' But Microsoft only had access to typefaces in the Monotype library, and couldn't ship any of Adobe's or Linotype's fonts in its programs. Palatino, for example, Connare's early favourite and one of the most popular faces at the time, was unavailable, with Microsoft making do with a less attractive clone called Book Antiqua. Connare worked on a team facilitating the types

Tahoma

Verdana

Georgia

Arial

Microsoft's other offerings: none of them caused a fuss.

Tahoma, Verdana and Georgia, all designed by Matthew Carter to replicate existing types elsewhere, and he used Arial as a competitor to Helvetica when working on something called Microsoft Web TV, enabling a user to connect their TV to the Internet, a precursor to the Amazon Fire Stick. 'The budget they had for buying in and making type was huge,' Connare recalls. 'Some of the programs they acquired cost virtually nothing, $500 or so, but we would be paying $100,000 for some typefaces.'

And then towards the end of 1994 Connare saw an almost-finished version of a piece of educational software called Microsoft Bob.

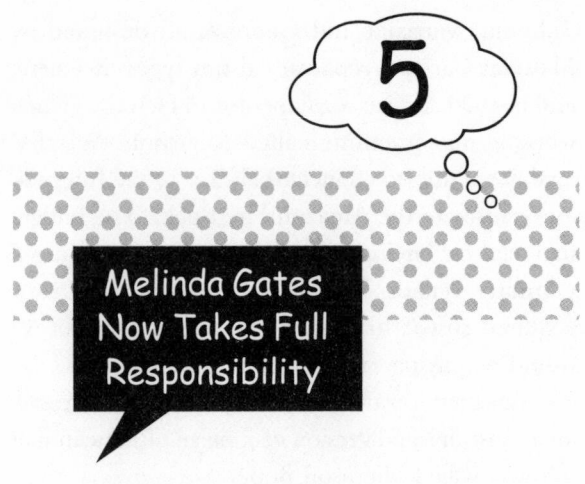

5

Melinda Gates Now Takes Full Responsibility

Microsoft Bob was designed to revolutionise computing for those who found computing hard going. It had the tone of the school lesson about it, a colourful series of rooms drawn by someone who found drawing hard going. Each room – a living room, a kitchen and in some versions an attic – contained objects a user could click on, including a calendar, a pad and paper, and a computer, and when they did so they'd be taken to software designed for that task (a calendar, word processor, a finance package, etc). To hold the user's hand, two animated figures, a dog named Rover and a paperclip named Clippy, would pop up with speech bubbles of helpful advice.

One of the things Rover helped you with was customisation: you could, according to Rover's dialogue box onscreen, add 'swarms of excellent stuff' to any room, such as flowers and books, and you could add doors 'that lead wherever you want'. Rover's guidance eliminated the need for a user manual, which new computer users either loathed or ignored anyway. And every now and then he barked, or at least said 'bow-wow!'

Bob's marketing manager was Melinda French, later Melinda Gates, a rising star at Microsoft involved in the launch of a number of high-profile products. Many years later, when her principal concerns had switched from tech to health and philanthropy in the developing world, Microsoft Bob was still on her mind. Addressing an audience of school children, she would call Microsoft Bob 'an utter and complete failure'. On another occasion, in a speech to a convention of successful women in business in 2017, she would again use Microsoft Bob as an example of something that, although unsuccessful, only made her try harder at other things; this time the failure was 'spectacular'.

Why was it so bad? It required a lot of memory to work efficiently, more than most home computers had installed. A reviewer for the *Washington Post* found that Clippy and Rover were more annoying than cute, its concept 'pre-adolescent' and 'brainless', and its look 'as lifeless as the fake cobwebs with which you can "decorate" your space'. *Time* magazine named it among the fifty worst inventions of all time, alongside New Coke, Smell-o-Vision and subprime mortgages. And there was another problem in the way it looked (beyond what the *New York Times* called the work of an 'aesthetically challenged

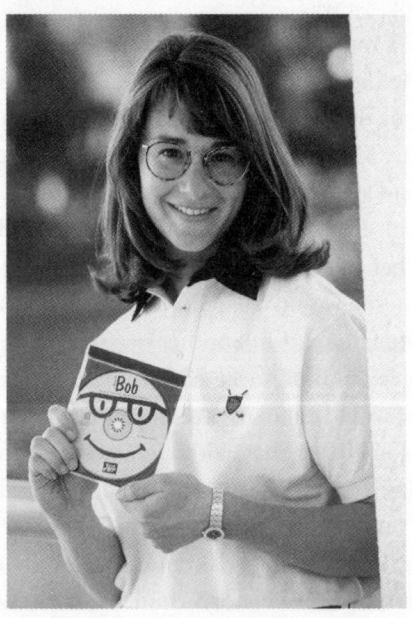

Before it failed: Melinda French still in upbeat mood with Microsoft Bob.

sixth-grader'). The typeface someone had cho-
sen to transmit Rover's speech bubbles was Times
New Roman. Times New Roman is the safest bet
of all, and usually bulletproof. It is suited to most
situations, but it did not suit the young and homely
feel of this new software; it made it look staid and
overwhelmingly dull, and it would remind its users
of textbooks.

Melinda French always told her audiences that,
against the odds, Microsoft Bob had an unexpected
'leave-behind' (i.e. 'result'). This was Comic Sans,
she explained, 'which I hear many people still dis-
cuss and some use'. This is slightly misleading, as
Comic Sans never appeared in Microsoft Bob. Not
that its designer didn't try his best to include it.

Vincent Connare has written about the saga on
his website. He had seen a beta version of Microsoft
Bob, and saw immediately how unsuitable its type
looked. Rover looked like a scamp, and everything
he said – 'To start a program just click on it … What
shall I add to your home?' – should have been in
something friendlier, perhaps even something that
looked like it was written by hand. Connare had
recently had some experience of sourcing and creating fonts for Microsoft software aimed specifically
at children, 'fonts looking like pizza, monsters and
ones with snow.'

Connare was a fan of comics and graphic novels, and started to look at books in his office, including *Batman: The Dark Knight Returns* by Frank Miller and the subversive superhero drama *Watchmen* by Alan Moore, Dave Gibbons and John Higgins. 'I took care not to copy the letters, but looked at varying shapes in differing styles.' Most comics used only capital letters, so he found limited inspiration for his lower-case alphabet. He emphasised the rounded corners available in the drawing tool Fontographer 'and drew the letters over and over again in the program until I got the shape I wanted'.

Connare's work resulted in a set of letters rather than a complete font, and for a while it didn't even have a name. The letters were not uniformly spaced, and carried elements that in a formal typeface would be considered unacceptable: p wasn't a mirror-opposite of q, for example. The form of the letters is not consistent: the size and shape of the bowls with B or R, for example, or within b or o. And the absence of serif legs at the top or bottom of capital letters is a style rule proudly broken by the curious nick at the top of C and the broad serifs on the I. Drawing with a mouse, Connare achieved the look of a medium-thickness felt pen, and in the main this wonky alphabet suited its intended purpose, which was to make learning brighter.

Comic Sans

Aa Bb Cc Dd

Ee Ff Gg Hh

Ii Jj Kk Ll

Mm Nn Oo

Pp Qq Rr Ss

Tt Uu Vv Ww

Xx Yy Zz

'The initial idea took minutes,' Connare told me. 'I never thought it would be set in all-caps, so I didn't worry about how these weird shapes would work that way. It looks horrible in all caps. The joy for me was not making it right or perfect or straight. My boss Robert Norton looked at it and said, "You should fix this, you should fix that," but I said. "No, the p and the q are just different strokes, and I want to keep them separate." That was the creative culture at Microsoft – you just stuck to your guns. I hope that people get that it's not really a font. Somebody called it my handwriting, but it's not my handwriting either.'

Despite the speed of his work, Connare's new letters entered the Microsoft Bob program too late. The letters were too tall and too wide for the metrics already assigned for Times New Roman in the dialogue boxes. The software was launched with its old type at the Consumer Electronics Show in Las Vegas in early 1995, and initially received a warm response. Anything that helped people with the daunting task of handling a new computer with Microsoft software was seen as a worthwhile thing. Only when users and computer journalists got to handle it properly from the spring of that year did its shortcomings become apparent. By the end of 1995, with hugely disappointing sales, Melinda French and other Microsoft executives faced the inevitability of abandoning Bob, Rover and Clippy to their fates, and concentrating all their efforts on Windows 95. But by then, Comic Sans had escaped.

Having missed out on its original intention, Connare did then complete his font. Initially it was called Comic Book, which seemed to limit its uses. Not long after it was changed to Comic Sans (even though everyone acknowledged its occasional properties as a serif), Connare noticed that people at Microsoft started using it in two ways – internally in a lot of emails, particularly asking staff members to 'fun' events like birthday parties and softball days; and externally and commercially, in a new piece of software called MS MovieMaker (this also featured

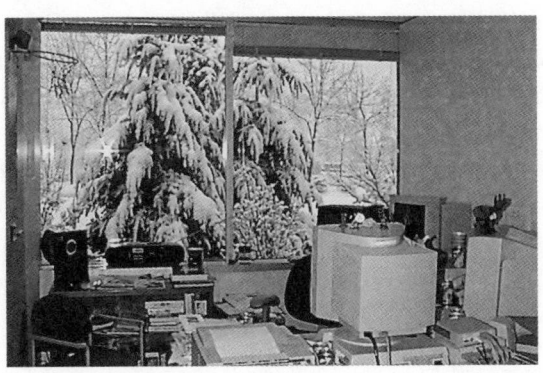

Creative chaos: the room where Comic Sans was born.

an animated element in its instruction). Then Comic Sans went wide, first in a bonus product to Windows 95, and soon after as a full-blown Windows 95 system font. And there it proved popular, predominantly because it didn't look remotely like anything else.

'The magic is that people took to it on their own,' says Tom Stephens, who worked alongside Connare in Microsoft's typography unit when Comic Sans emerged. 'It does get misused, usually because somebody just loves it. The fact that people have the freedom to say, "This is my favourite font and I'm going to use it" is a marvellous thing ... It's almost an anti-technology typeface: very casual, very welcoming. It's like going home, back to your childhood, getting letters from family members. Or somebody might use it to get away from the staid environment of their work. When you use Comic Sans, you're making a statement: "I'm more relaxed, more creative. I may be working in this area, but this job does not define me."'*

And then, Vincent Connare notes, the backlash began.

---

* As quoted in the *Guardian*, 28 March 2017.

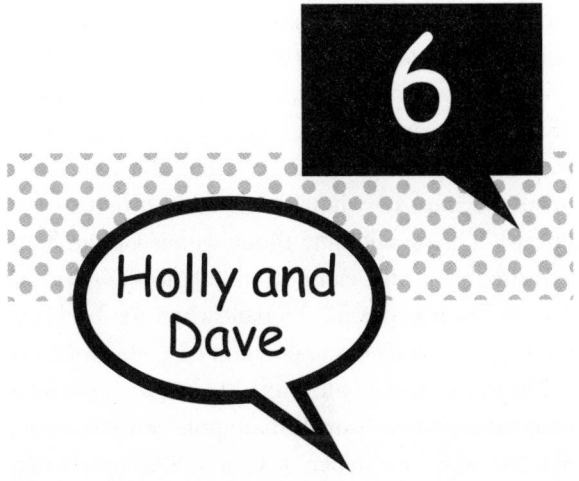

6

Holly and Dave

The backlash began because people liked Comic Sans too much. It became the 'Macarena' of fonts, the *Great British Bake Off* of fonts. It was something that people believed existed just for them, something they could understand. It was simple and warming, and maybe it reminded users of the colourful letters that doubled as fridge magnets. It was everything Vincent Connare had wanted it to be, apart from the fact that it had entered a global arena.

Or: it was the worst thing ever. Not only an insult to the drop-down-menu, but an insult to the heritage of print. It was a virus escaped from the lab. Type aficionados didn't like it, the way coffee connoisseurs didn't like Starbucks; it diluted everything they held dear. And it was being used everywhere on everything, as if letters had just been invented and Comic Sans was the only choice.

It is impossible to date when the perceived misuse began, or when those not attuned to the fineries of type etiquette thought that Comic Sans was suitable for the sides of ambulances and gravestones. But it is possible to date when the backlash itself became a media opportunity. For this we must credit the romantic allegiance of Dave and Holly Combs, a couple from Indianapolis who, in 2002, bonded over their dislike of Comic Sans being used all over.

The world must have been in a more stable place when such a harmless thing was worth such attention. But Holly Combs was a type enthusiast, and like many of this breed, cared passionately about an inconsistent p and q, or a badly spaced sign. The beginning of the end for her came when, tasked with developing a gallery at a local museum, she found that every sign was in a type she felt unsuitable. It 'felt just like a punch in the gut,' she remembered later.

Then she began spotting it elsewhere, used in equally unsuitable ways. It was a fun font that had been misinterpreted by those who had never had

access to type choices before. Before home computers and desktop publishing, such things had been
left to the professionals.* Even in the most suitable
of uses – essentially anything to do with children –
Holly Combs wasn't a fan. 'It's poorly designed. Its
strokes are irregular. It's a really ugly, comical, stupid, ugly font.' In another interview she exclaimed,
'I got a funeral announcement in Comic Sans. I
mean, that's sad! I don't want a funeral announcement in *Comic Sans*!'

Dave Combs, who shared this outrage but in a
more raised-eyebrow kind of way, suggested that
there was only one solution: there was no point com-
plaining, as things had already gone too far. So it had
to be banned. For the first time since Gutenberg, a
font was deemed so offensive that obliteration was
the only answer.**

Quite soon it had the whiff of book-burning
about it. But because this was the internet age, it also
had the whiff of irony about it. Or rather, because
this was the internet age – where a law stated that

---

* It was the same with burgeoning text language. There would always be
those who would end a condolence note with LOL.
** The couple emailed its creator to ask whether he wouldn't object to
their 'Ban Comic Sans' campaign. 'It seemed silly,' Vincent Connare
remembers, 'but I said knock yourselves out.'

no forum debate or Twitter spat may exist without someone quite soon comparing what was being discussed 'to Nazi Germany' – it had achieved those other great concatenations, the tipping point and the perfect storm: type+unforgivable-taste+gone-too-far-this-time+ban+T-shirts. Dave Combs did indeed print T-shirts and stickers and mugs with a logo ('Comic Sans' encased within an internationally recognised red Forbidden/No Entry sign), and the campaign was launched.

It was a slow burn. The first mention I can find in the national press is from 2004, some eighteen months after the campaign began, an article in Canada's *National Post* headlined 'Typeface of Disgrace'. 'It's a bad font,' the story begins. 'It makes its way into e-mails, newsletters, party invitations, school exams, even restaurant menus. Too many people have been hypnotized by its curves and easy-going manner, blind to its disgrace.' The first quote is from Dave Combs: using this font 'is like showing up to a black-tie event in a clown costume'. The writer of the story reached a conclusion: 'The font wars are raging on the World Wide Web.'

Similar stories followed. Most began with a variation of 'love it or loathe it, it ain't going away!' It was clear that the debate wasn't going away either, but there was a protracted lull. The next wave came five years later in April 2009, when the *Wall Street Journal* reported that 'Typeface inspired by Comic Books Has Become a Font of Ill Will'. By this point, the article explained, Comic Sans had spread to porn sites and 'hospital posters about bowel cancer'.

Three weeks later the story was picked up by the *Guardian*, which ran an editorial 'In Praise of Comic Sans', proposing a backlash against the backlash. By this time, the font had spread to Internet cafes in Nepal and beach towels in Australia.

Most of this paper is in Guardian Egyptian,
but in the interests of typographical diversity
the two words above in blue are in Comic Sans.
Look closely, for this is a typeface under attack.
Designers hate Comic Sans, for it undercuts
the sanctity of their craft. Font fundamentalists
attack offending signs with angry stickers. And
there is naturally enough a Facebook group called
Ban Comic Sans … [But] it can be a welcome
break from those corporate Arials and oh-so-chic
Helveticas.

This set a new trend. People began popping their heads above the bunkers. 'Typographers will cringe,' wrote Patrick Kingsley in the *Guardian* in June 2010, 'but I've always had a soft spot for Comic Sans.' The

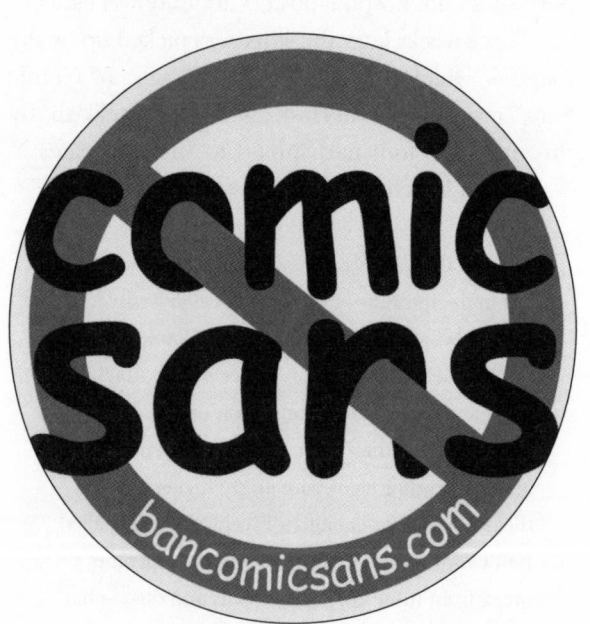

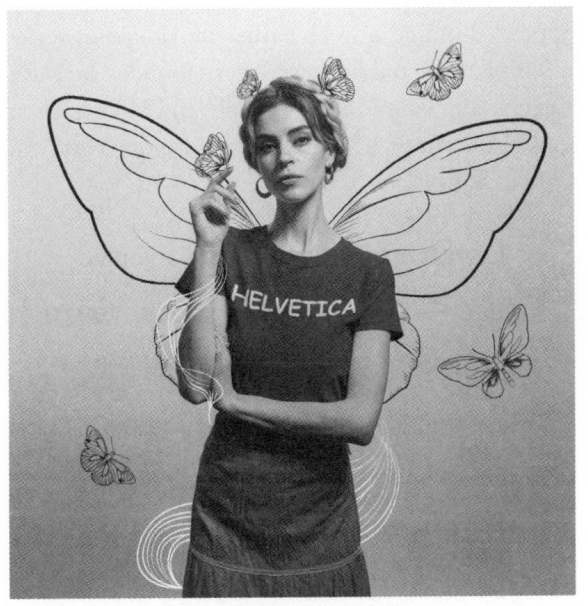

She's no angel: Comic Sans masquerading as another famous face.

writer talked to Holly Combs, who had an oddly familiar refrain: 'Using Comic Sans is like turning up to a black-tie event in a clown costume.'

The most propulsive defence of the font had appeared online a week earlier in *McSweeney's*, the multi-platform publishing concern founded by Dave Eggers. 'I'm Comic Sans, Asshole', by Mike Lacher, took the form of a 'short imagined monologue' (in Comic Sans):

Listen up. I know the shit you've been saying behind my back. You think I'm stupid. You think I'm immature. You think I'm a malformed, pathetic excuse for a font. Well think again, nerdhole, because I'm Comic Sans, and I'm the best thing to happen to typography since Johannes fucking Gutenberg.

You don't like that your coworker used me on that note about stealing her yogurt from the break room fridge? You don't like that I'm all over your sister-in-law's blog? You don't like that I'm on the sign for that new Thai place? You think I'm pedestrian and tacky? Guess the fuck what, Picasso. We don't all have seventy-three weights of stick-up-my-ass Helvetica sitting on our seventeen-inch MacBook Pros. Sorry the entire world can't all be done in stark Eurotrash Swiss type. Sorry some people like to have fun.

Sorry I'm standing in the way of your minimalist Bauhaus-esque fascist snoozefest.

And on like that for a bit, until Comic Sans decides to 'go get hammered with Papyrus'.

And then (because no story about Comic Sans would sit still for long) came the backlash against the backlash against the backlash. In December 2010, a 21-year-old graphic design student at the University of Portsmouth named Mike Dempsey made a website called Comic Sans Criminal. This was a calm and elegant site advocating a little restraint. Comic Sans was fine in the correct circumstances, it argued, but these circumstances were limited ('When your audience is under 11 years old; when you're designing a comic'). As before, you shouldn't use it 'in a doctor's diagnosis letter'.

But the strength of the site lies in a pledge that visitors may fill in and print, and in a rebuke you may email to others about misuse. 'I .... (the undersigned),' the pledge begins. '… understand that my choice of font has the power to subconsciously and incorrectly set the tone for a piece of printed material, and as a result promise to seriously consider whether Comic Sans is an appropriate font choice before using it in any printed work in the future. Signed ....'

The project was part of Dempsey's degree 'and was only ever intended to be seen by a couple of tutors for a couple of minutes'. And things would have stayed that way had he not posted the draft version of his project on Dribbble, a site that publishes work in progress for critique from other graphic designers. Someone copied the link to Twitter, where it immediately trended, and in turn attracted more than 200,000 unique visitors to Dempsey's website in two days. It received a much greater global response than the ventures produced by others on his course. 'The brief was to create a piece of work that highlighted an issue you felt passionately about,' Dempsey explained. 'Some chose more serious issues like poverty, alcoholism, world hunger, etc … '*

As ever with this typeface, the big noise was the light relief. Fifteen years after its release, its 'very human' shape of an a and the errant lip of a swiftly drawn C still brought the heat. It showed the power of *something*: an alphabet; the playful nature of writers who knew a good diversion when they saw one;

---

* ComicSansCriminal.com is still partially active. There are no stickers or T-shirts available, and the link to 'Alternative Comic Book Fonts' is defunct, but you can still send a rebuke to someone.

'Hey Simon!' read an email I sent myself from the site. 'Your friend Simon Garfield thinks you're a Comic Sans Criminal!

'"A Comic Sans what?"' I hear you ask.

'Well, a Comic Sans Criminal is someone who uses Comic Sans inappropriately, and it has been suggested that you may indeed be guilty of this atrocious typographic crime! We seriously suggest you visit ComicSansCriminal.com to begin your rehabilitation. We look forward to meeting the new, typographically aware you!'

the polemical slap of social media. An unexpected quality of Comic Sans, like the comic book heroes who inspired it, is its vulnerability, a feeling that it is never really in charge of its fate. This is its super-power. There's an appealing photograph of Holly and Dave Combs from 2019 in which they are both wearing black T-shirts. Hers reads 'ban comic sans' (in Comic Sans), his reads 'Be a nice human.' (in in-offensive and comfortable cursive). They both have mischief on their faces, as if, anytime soon, they might absolutely change their minds.

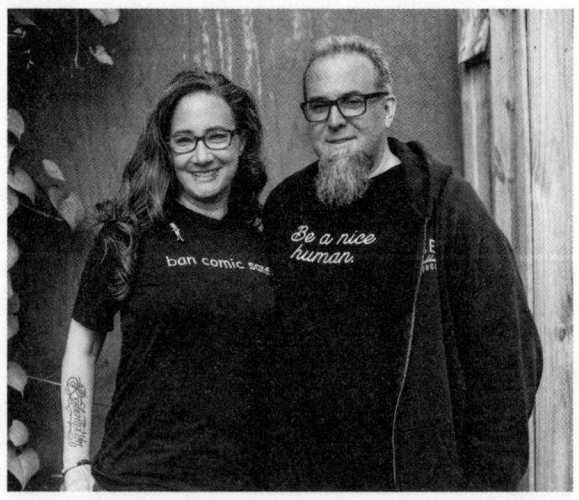

A shared love, a shared hate: Holly and Dave Combs launch a campaign.

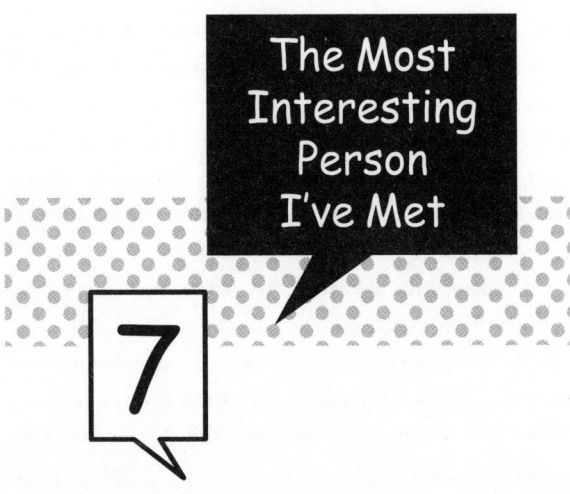

The Most Interesting Person I've Met

7

'I live between Nice and Marseille,' Connare tells me on our first Zoom chat. 'About an hour up from the coast. Life is much better here.'

Connare was sixty-two when we spoke. His hair is almost completely white. He's wearing a green Adidas hoodie. One of the posters behind him, from the 1965 Cannes Film Festival, shows Marilyn Monroe blowing out a candle on a cake.

He lives here with his wife Sue Rider, who serves as agent/manager for the physicist Professor Brian Cox. They lived in England for several years, and had a holiday home in France, but moved for good after Brexit. They have cats. He plays a lot of tennis and paints and photographs. During the Covid-19 lockdowns he improved his French, learnt car maintenance and built a pétanque court. They have fifty olive trees, yielding about ten gallons of oil a year. 'The first year we gave a lot of it away, which was a mistake, because you then don't have enough for yourself.'

I asked him whether he got bored of talking about Comic Sans.

'In France people tend not to talk about what they do. If I do get asked, and I tell them I've done TrueType hinting* most of my life they're not that interested. So I say, "I made typefaces," and they say, "Have I heard of any?"'

'"Comic Sans?"'

'"Oh yeah. I love it!" They always tell me they love it and they use it all the time.

'And people say, "I can't believe I met the man who made Comic Sans!" One man kept going on about it. He was a little bit *too* excited about it. I met Tim Minchin when he was doing *Matilda*, and was introduced by someone from the BBC as "He made Comic Sans," and Tim Minchin goes, "You're the most interesting person I've met all night!"'

---

* The process of hinting, in this case in Apple's TrueType format, involves improving a font's legibility onscreen.

Connare left Microsoft with stock options in 1999, at a point when Comic Sans MS (as it was officially called) was neither a controversial choice nor a target of ridicule. If you liked it, good for you, and if you didn't, also good for you. (Perhaps you would rather choose Trebuchet MS, another of Connare's designs. Trebuchet, from 1996, shared its name with a model of French catapult, and was again designed to fix a problem, specifically how to inject energy and personality into a new sans face that works onscreen as both a display font and at much smaller sizes for text and low resolutions.)*

After Microsoft, Connare went back to school, enrolling in a one-year master's in type design at the University of Reading. One may detect a certain

---

* At Trebuchet's launch, Microsoft explained why it took its place as a core system font in both Windows and Internet Explorer. It praised the 'engineering' of his lower-case g and upper-case M, reminiscent of some of Paul Renner's alternate designs for Futura. 'Less noticeable details include the serif-like bars of the lowercase i and j, and the curled, kicking stem of the lowercase l.' A year later, Connare was part of the team that designed Webdings, a font that included 230 popular 'Web-related' images or dingbats, an early version of what we would later call emojis. These included simple black-and-white images of cars and other forms of transport, computers and other tech, and many human activities such as swimming, skiing and shouting. One image in particular became associated with Connare: the 'levitating man', a man in a suit and tie floating serenely. Connare has said he was inspired by the image on the 2 Tone record label, which was itself modelled on a photo of the reggae musician Peter Tosh. In Webdings on Microsoft Word, you'll still get levitating man by keying lower-case 'm'.

poignancy here – the desire of a man who had made one of the most notorious fonts in the world to learn how academia dealt the cards; the notion of a man who had worked at the most successful software company in the world now reading about type history. Caroline Archer-Parré, who would soon become the world expert in Baskerville, was doing her PhD at Reading at the same time.

In 2001 Connare began working with the type designer Bruno Maag at his company Dalton Maag, and when he told outsiders about his projects, for McDonald's and Nokia, everyone still wanted to know about Microsoft and Comic Sans. 'I spoke at

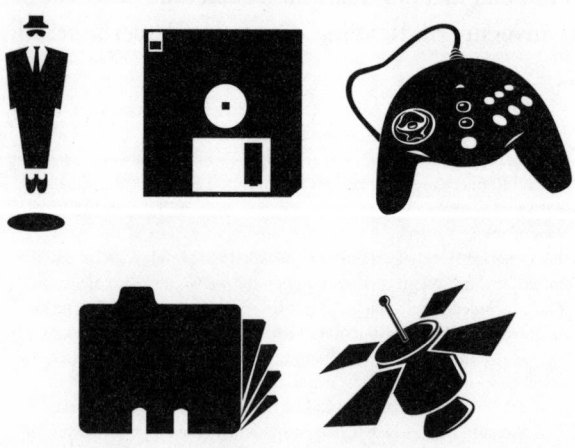

Webdings: the levitating man and other dingbats from the floppy disc era.

the *Wired* conference and I was told not to mention anything apart from the Microsoft days. Now I'm only being asked to talk about Comic Sans, but it's better not to be asked at all.' (The *Wired* conference in 2015 conferred a quasi-rock star status on Connare; Comic Sans was now folklore, its standing within popular culture iconic, its standing in the type world irrelevant. To confirm his position, Greg Williams, *Wired*'s deputy editor, took him for a spin in a revamped Jaguar XF for a promotional video. 'His approach to design is all about human interaction,' Williams said of Connare on the voiceover, 'enhancing the way we communicate with the technology we depend on. In a similar way this car has been completely redesigned to better understand the driver.')

After our conversation, Connare sent me an email with photographs. The first was a certificate headed 'The Palmer Method of Business Handwriting'. 'This Certifies that Vincent Connare has attained a degree of excellence in the Palmer Method of Muscular Movement Business Writing and is entitled to this Student's Certificate for proficiency in Rapid Legible Handwriting.' The date was 1936; it was his father's, from a time when calligraphy was seen as essential professional tool. The son inherited this belief. After Dalton Maag, Connare enrolled for a PhD in handwriting at Birmingham City University, where Caroline Archer-Parré was now teaching. 'I thought it was romantic to have beautiful handwriting, but I found that the reason we don't do it is because society has changed and we don't need it anymore.'

Connare also sent me a picture of a slide he used as an opener in his PowerPoint talks. It showed a vintage calligraphy pen with a metal nib alongside a cup of espresso, and a swashbuckling inscription on paper that the pen had written with the coffee: 'I made Comic Sans'.

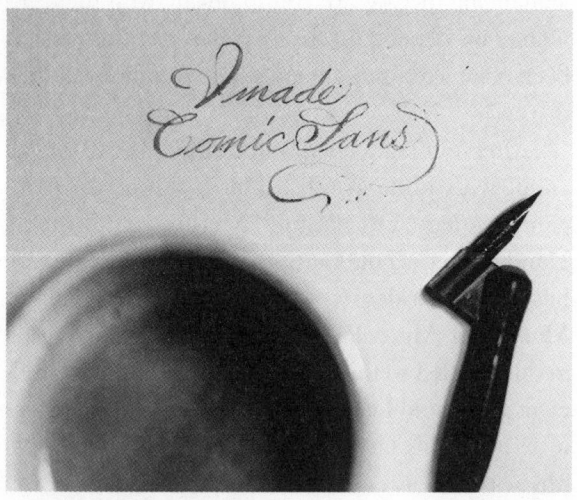

Coffee, meet calligraphy: Vincent Connare writes his legacy in espresso.

He receives no royalties from his creation. 'You were paid to produce things for Microsoft. If you looked at Adobe products there were huge lists of names in the "about" boxes – a list of everyone who had worked on that thing. But in any Microsoft product there's nobody's name on anything. Bill Gates didn't want to make people famous. One, because they might be courted and leave, and two because it all belonged to him anyway. Royalties would have been nice, but nobody has ever made any proper money off a type.'

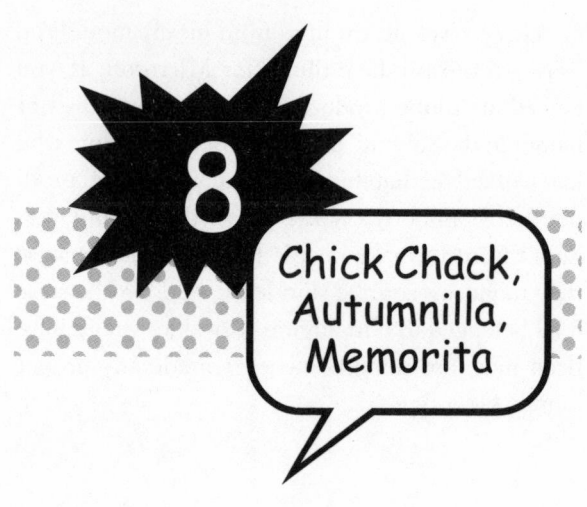

8

Chick Chack,
Autumnilla,
Memorita

But they keep on trying. Every few days I get an
email from MyFonts, a digital typeface distribu-
tor owned by Monotype. Its Deals of the Week
always contain tempting bargains. In April 2023,
for example, I could have snapped up Campeche,
inspired by the playful spirit of Latin America, especially suitable for packaging, branding and editorial layouts, available in a great many variations
of widths and weights, down from $239 to $96.50.
That was some big deal – maybe too big (I would
have got Campeche Condensed Thin, Campeche
Condensed ExtraLight, Campeche Condensed

Light, Campeche Condensed Regular, Campeche Condensed Medium, Campeche Condensed SemiBold, Campeche Condensed Bold, Campeche Condensed Black, Campeche Condensed Heavy, and forty-five more that weren't condensed, such as Campeche Expanded SemiBold and Campeche Display Expanded Medium). If I was just looking for a straightforward, natural script type, I could have downloaded Rosttaly Script, available in just three fonts – Regular, Italic or Underline – half the normal price at $12. Or then there was the unique one-font solution of Fastlynk Regular – jagged and sharp, a great boy racer, something one might see whooshing by from a window of a speeding train. Fastlynk Regular has motion in its DNA, claimed its creators Abdul Malik Wisnu and Anyang Fibriyanto, and seems like a good deal at $16.10 down from $23.*

Connare was right: the designers of each of these types would do well to have day jobs, as none of them featured in the MyFonts annual list of top ten sellers. Although, to his credit, cumulatively Abdul Malik Wisnu might be doing OK, as he'll also be

---

* Monotype Imaging Holdings Inc., based in Woburn, Massachusetts, is the monolithic digital typesetting company that now owns or manages the bulk of the English-speaking world's digital foundries, including MyFonts, ITC, Linotype, Bitstream, Fontshop and Hoefler & Co. For more on its hot-metal heritage see the first book in this series, *Albertus*.

gathering a royalty from his five hundred other font families, including Crash Soul, a handwritten brush script, Redzein, a vintage display slab, and Suntage, a vintage 'wild west' sans.

Where do these crazy names come from? All these names from Wisnu like Cronisse, Costiera, Magicher, Kavaloora and Lordcorps? They come from the vast but slowly dwindling pool of names (real, imagined and composite) that are as yet unclaimed, unregistered, suggestive and inoffensive. That pool level was a little higher until Wisnu claimed Chick Chack, Autumnilla, Memorita and Winterline. You wanted to name your great new character set Avocado Creamy? Too late – it's gone!

An email from MyFonts in April 2023 announces yet another new design, and this time its creators have excelled themselves: it's called Penis. Had to happen, I suppose. And of course it comes in many sizes, extra thin condensed and bold extra wide among them. Unfortunately, I look a little closer and find it is not Penis but Premis.

Premis is not as good, though it has its own selling points. It looks a little like Helvetica, and hopes to be as versatile. It claims to be 'universal and neutral on the one hand, and distinctive and special on the other', and its three Finnish creators playfully recreated its design process for prospective purchasers:

> 'That letter r is absolutely cool. Should we take the same angularity for f and t as well?' asked Erik Bertell.

> 'Yeah, this one could use a little extra love. Small Caps, huh?' said his brother Emil Bertell.

> 'With the cutting of those ends, I wouldn't be so mathematically precise to cut everything to the same level. The letter c especially becomes vague,' observed their friend Teo Tuominen.

MyFonts also sells Comic Sans, but this is less of a bargain. You will get four fonts – Regular, Bold, Italic and Bold Italic – for $129, which might seem pricey when you consider that the first two already come free with Apple Pages and Microsoft Word. And it has a lot of competition from other, cheaper fonts with comic-adjacent attributes, with names such as Comic Hero, Comic Geek, Comic Impact and Comicbasic, fonts that look like they've been designed swiftly and simply, perhaps with a thick felt pen or crayon, ready to go out into the world to please a lot of people. A search on MyFonts reveals

11,686 results for 'Comic', which clearly needs to be narrowed down. 'Comic book' yields 600 choices, while 'cartoon font' yields 192, among them Hello Melky (nice and fat with an outline), Lovely Scream Queens (chunky, paper cut-out), and Rumley Moon (hipsterish, waxy, lava lamp).

Other digital type foundries, including Fontshop and ITC, have their own deep comic-style selection. Which makes the extraordinary fame and popularity of Comic Sans even more extraordinary. I would wager that of all the 11,686 comic-related fonts on MyFonts, very few people, apart from the designers and a few of the designers' friends, have heard of Comic Pro JY, Comiccrazy, or Comic Sidekick, or are able to recognise them on a poster.

One reason for the success of Comic Sans is that a version of it was available on many people's first computer. It was so blatantly different from Baskerville and Times New Roman that it just had to be sampled. And its non-type simplicity spawned notoriety, and then controversy, and typefaces (like everything else in a crowded market) do love a narrative. The fact that users immediately identified it with fun and children provided that other key element in type selection: association. A better question, perhaps, is why all the *others* exist. Why, for instance, do we have Comicbon? What value does Comicblast impart? Is it possible to say, in a philistine argument one might also use against novels and paintings (and books about design), why we need more of the same? More precisely, why do we need 'over 230,000 fonts, and counting' on offer at MyFonts, and the several hundreds of thousands available elsewhere? In other words, are there simply too many type-faces? Because we certainly thought so a century ago.

In September 1929, the American Typographers Association annual convention decided to create a board 'to pass judgment on all new type faces of-fered from either domestic or foreign sources, and to recommend such faces as are in their judgment of value to the art of typography and the science of advertising'. It was a putsch of sorts, a mild re-bellion against the preponderance of new trends in type that, if not unchecked, might render small printworks and type houses bankrupt. The elabo-rate designs created in New York such as Bernhard Gothic, Broadway and Ultra Bodoni were jostling for rack space with popular geometric sans serif ar-rivals from Germany such as Futura and Kabel, and any client with an advertising budget couldn't get enough of new art deco or so-called 'modernistic' styles. Even in the 1920s there was no limit to how tall, sharp or rounded a display type could get.

The problems for the American Typographers Association were clear: its members didn't know when either the demands or temptations would stop. If type suppliers and printers didn't have the latest models in stock, orders would go elsewhere. But this year's model had its obsolescence built in; unlike Futura, most types weren't built to last, for where are your 1920s Edinas, Messe-Grotesks and Blanchards now? (Blanchard was last sighted on the sleeve of Alice Cooper's single 'School's Out' in 1972; Messe-Grotesk was last seen on a booklet promoting the Mittelrheinisches Musikfest in Trier in 1925.)

Buying a set of metal types in many styles and sizes was a significant investment; there were no instant-download MyFonts-style bargains to be had. And so meetings were held to try to determine what would and wouldn't last, what were the best faces for every job. Who would decide on these important matters? No less than the National Board of Legible Type Faces for Advertising Purposes. Its aim was to determine if new typefaces were "worthy of endorsement as to legibility, beauty, and suitability for advertising use".

The minutes from these meetings, held in the early 1930s, range from the ludicrous to the hilarious, and when the type historian Paul Shaw tracked them down in 2007 he observed that the board's true intention 'was to praise "classical" typefaces and condemn "modernistic" ones, thereby absolving type houses from the responsibility of having to purchase the latter'. Things would obviously be cheaper that way. The Great Depression was hitting the type industry as hard as any other, and as with almost all arts at all times, a fearful establishment would do what it could to defend the past against the future.

The board first met at the National Republican Club in New York in January 1930. Early discussion focused on a design created by Morris Fuller Benton in 1929, the chunkiest typeface ever to have graced Times Square, the epitome of American art deco:

CHAIRMAN: Let us take the Broadway
Condensed. My feeling on Broadway is that it has
done its turn and it is off the stage.

MEMBER: You can go farther and say it never
should have been on.

MEMBER: Even good taste condemns that.

MEMBER: Mr. Chairman, before we leave Broadway, I would like to say that the typographers have spent a great deal of money and have gotten very little out of it.

MEMBER: It was a perfect fizzle. We made a Gallia that came out at the same time. Gallia is the twin sister of Broadway. [Made in 1927 by Wadsworth A. Parker, it was indeed another grandstand of a design, all swash, fancy and Roaring Twenties; today you'd see it used by a company renting a vintage Rolls Royce for a wedding.]

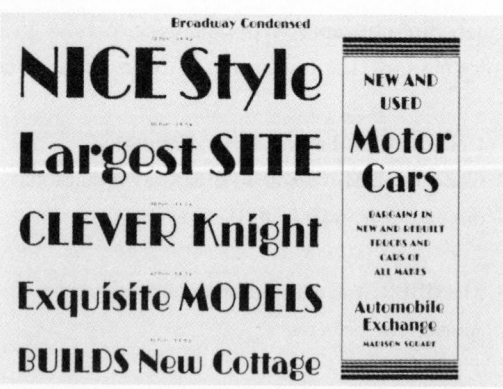

The glamorous 1920s: Broadway Condensed ready for its spotlight.

MEMBER: I think that is quite encouraging. I was afraid it was going to be a success.

MEMBER: It is really amazing that the American Type Founders should have made the Broadway Condenser [*sic*].

MEMBER: We could do this: We could tell them to make one face and stop there. I mean instead of expanding it, condensing it, and putting high hats on it.

MEMBER: Take the Gallia. You say it has gone out. I knew after six months that was going to look stale, but it was a little novelty while it lasted, like a lot of styles we have in neckties, or anything else …

The meeting pursued its censorial manner for quite a while, dismissively considering several other faces, and suggesting that there should now be a three-tier classification system for all typefaces: classic types that 'conform with the best tradition of the arts' (i.e. Caslon and Baskerville); those with 'novelty appeal', their resilience as yet unknown (Futura); and types with 'no reason for existence' that one member suggested should be classified as 'freakish'.

Amusing as this was, it was almost all hot air. Broadway is still available as a system font on the Microsoft Word drop-down menu, and even now nothing says cigar-chewing impresario quite like it. Had the board's classification system stood, where, thirty years later, would they have placed the colossally intrusive Helvetica or the typewriter imitations of Courier? And one certainly would have feared for the fate of freakish Comic Sans.* (Although Comic Sans being Comic Sans, it would have confounded all expectations and bounced over all opprobrium, going from reviled to novelty to classic in about twenty years.)

*

You know it's a classic when it gets a revival. In 2014 Comic Sans was spruced up as Comic Neue by Craig Rozynski and Hrant Papazian, who claimed

---

* *Print* magazine, where this story first appeared, clearly didn't agree that there could ever be too many types, although it too regularly offered its own selection of favoured designs, a task it took seriously: in 2016, for example, the selection panel choosing the Best New Typefaces of the Year consisted of twenty-three aficionados. They chose, among others, Action Condensed, Equitan Sans and Equitan Slab, Triade and Kopius.

on their website that it would make your lemonade stand look like a Fortune 500 company.

'Comic Neue aspires to be the casual script choice for everyone including the typographically savvy,' Rozynski claimed. 'The squashed, wonky, and weird glyphs of Comic Sans have been beaten into shape while maintaining the honesty that made Comic Sans so popular. It's perfect as a display face, for marking up comments, and writing passive-aggressive office memos.'

It came in two cuts: Comic Neue and Comic Neue Angular, the latter almost completely eradicating the curving human playfulness of the original into something engineered by a machine. Vincent Connare didn't care for the update much, suggesting it should all be 'more casual'. In recent years, partly due to a crowdfunding campaign, new versions of Comic Neue have included support for more than forty languages, including Esperanto. It certainly stayed true to its roots in one sense: it was never at risk of taking itself too seriously. At the foot of its launch website it quoted a comment from HuffPost Tech: 'It's shite. Someone created a slightly less horrible version of Comic Sans.'

Five years later, an even less less-horrible version appeared called Comic Code. This was a monospaced revival (where almost all the characters took up the same amount of horizontal space), and what its creator called 'an unapologetic admittance of Comic Sans's positives'. Spending $100 at ILoveTypography.com would get you Comic Code Ultra Light Italic, Comic Code Light, Comic Code Light Italic, Comic Code Ligatures Thin, Comic Code Ligatures Medium Italic, and more than twenty other variations. In each style, the alphabet looks similar to the original but neater and calmer (less like the writing of a child, and more like the writing of a pedantic and less erratic adult).

It was the work of Toshi Omagari, the Japanese designer who had revived Albertus and other types by Berthold Wolpe at Monotype in 2017. At its launch, Omagari explained how he had wanted to make something specifically legible for computer

Comic Code
+ Comic Code Ligatures

Monospaced interpretation of the most over-hated typeface

programming, 'which is a corner of typography that involves intensive typing that feels more akin to handwriting than typesetting'. That, of course, was Vincent Connare's starting point too.

'Let's face it,' Omagari reasoned, 'sometimes professional appearance is exactly what you don't want. Comic Sans resonates because it doesn't talk down to you while making its message clearly heard with legible letters.' He now wanted to improve its spacing and outline, and hoped to help coders achieve a sense of flow while working, 'a literal manifestation of "code like nobody's watching".'

'It seems to be very popular, at least on screen,' Omagari told me. 'On paper the outlines always look terrible, and I can't really defend that, but on screen it looks great thanks to really nice pixelation and manual hinting [a process whereby outlines of characters are carefully distorted to better fit a pixel grid]. My version is Comic Sans-based, but it's much more legible, and more comfortable to use. And people seemed to notice, which restores my faith in people's eyes.'

I asked whether he had to obtain approval from Microsoft to amend it in this way. 'I did ask Microsoft if they're going to be bothered and they said no. But no permission was needed. Microsoft has no copyright on the word 'Comic', and the new outlines are all drawn from scratch. 'I think I showed the early design to Vincent, and he seemed delighted and puzzled at the same time.'

When I asked Vincent Connare what he thought about it now, he said, 'I remember seeing it but I didn't pay that much attention to it. I understand it though – he was solving a problem the same way I was.'

Fulfilling a need, fixing a problem – these do seem to be the best answers yet to the question 'Why so many types?'

Almost a century ago the German calligrapher and type designer Jan Tschichold composed an influential rationalist manifesto in which sans serif faces were everything, the reader was rendered a 'passive' viewer, and decadence was rejected in favour of the straightforward transmission of meaning and legibility (he later acknowledged how these principles unwittingly came across as fascistic). His manifesto was deemed timely and necessary, not least because of the greatly increased amount of printing materials confronting the modern consumer, and the increase in type choices required to transmit them. In the 1920s the world was simply moving too fast. People once had 'plenty of time to read line by line in a leisurely manner', but now 'as a rule we no longer read quietly ... but glance quickly over the whole, and only if our interest is awakened do we study it in detail'.*

So now simplicity and clarity were paramount, both in the look of a type and its congenial relationship with others. For this, new types were required, and would continue to be required in any age professing to be modern. 'Though its significance

---

* *Die neue Typographie*, published in Berlin in 1928. A translation by Ruari McLean published by the University of California Press appeared in 1995. In the late 1940s Tschichold created a unified design for Penguin Books.

remains undeniable,' Jan Tschichold reasoned, 'to think today that the Gutenberg Bible represents an achievement that can never again be reached is both naive and romantic rubbish. If we want to "prove ourselves worthy" of the clearly significant achievements of the past, we must set our own achievements beside them born out of our own time. They can only become "classic" if they are unhistoric.'

This is another reason we need so many types, and why Comic Sans fitted right in: like Futura, Gill Sans and Helvetica before it, it was a type of its age. Purists may still balk at the comparison with these stalwarts, but the roots of its success are similar: it met a singular need, and then a popular demand, albeit an unintended and unsophisticated one. Typefaces are the clothes that words wear; fashion suits the times. Comic Sans arrived at precisely the right time, as Microsoft word processing entered the home. And it was not a revival of anything, unless it was a thought revival of the way its users remembered writing and reading as children.

In 1930, two years after Jan Tschichold, Stanley Morison wrote what immediately became another standard text, *First Principles of Typography*. He observed how 'Type design moves at the pace of the most conservative reader. The good type designer therefore realises that, for a new fount to be successful, it has to be so good that only very few recognise its novelty.'

Hardly the case with Comic Sans, of course, either in its critical reception or its take-up; by this reasoning it could only be howled at by the cognoscenti. Morison, the typographic advisor at Monotype and the driving force behind Times New Roman, could hardly be considered closed to innovation. But he would have felt very queasy at the sight of that errant serif at the top of the C or that wobbly jelly of the m. He went on: 'If my friends think that the tail of my lower-case r or the lip of my lower-case e is rather jolly, you may know that the fount would have been better had neither been made.'

In 1995 the type historian Sebastian Carter again considered the need for new faces, and by then there were many more of them. The principles of type applied to the purest creation of other objects too:

> We see highly simplified classics of design – a chair by Marcel Breuer, a fork by Arne Jacobsen, or Paul Renner's Futura typeface – and we wonder why anything else is required. But then we experience a natural revulsion, and embrace variety, experiment and amusement, even if it sometimes leads to kitsch. After a while we swing back again to purity.

In everyone but a few single-minded zealots there reside both the puritan and the pluralist.*

And there is yet one more reason for the new types that appear each week in my emails from MyFonts and Fontshop (in April 2023 alone I was offered the ultra condensed poster-perfect DxSlight, the sharp and dashing text type Certiveit, and the handwritten brush style of Destroy, ideal for coffee shops and good-vibes logos). The reason is joy. Looking back on his work as an inspirational calligrapher and type designer in pre-war Germany, Rudolf Koch wrote that the making of letters was for him 'the purest and greatest pleasure, and at many stages of my life it was to me what a song is to the singer, a picture to the painter, a shout to the elated, or a sigh to the oppressed – it was and is for me the most happy and perfect expression of my life.'**

---

* From *Twentieth Century Type Designers*, 2nd edition, published by Lund Humphries in 1995.
** Both Koch and Stanley Morison are featured in the first book in this series, *Albertus*.

When I met the leading young type designer Lynne Yun in New York, I asked her a similar question. Too many types? She looked at me in the way Paul McCartney might if I'd asked him to stop at 'Love Me Do'. My question was clearly nonsensical, for it would suggest a cessation of human progress. Besides, she reasons in a Zen-like way, 'people make new typefaces because they can't stop making them'. Yun was weeks away from releasing Felicette, her latest sans serif, a friendly, charming and contemporary face she describes as 'elegant, lovable

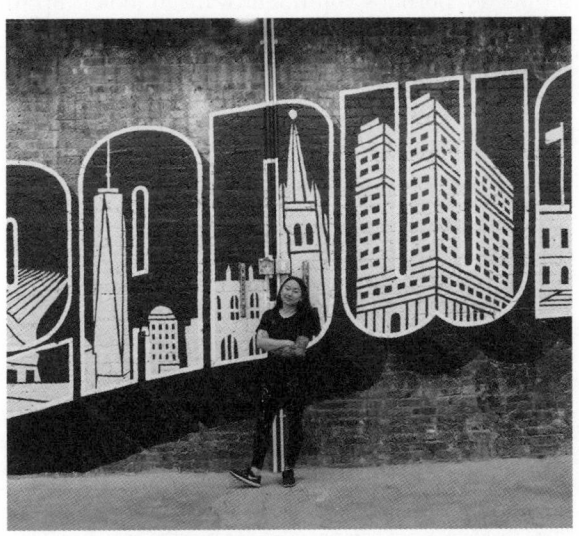

'Made by real people': Lynne Yun by her Broadway mural.

and good-looking – just like Félicette, its namesake Parisian cat who was sent into space'.

Yun is a committed type educator. She spent much of the pandemic recording a series of free video tutorials about the fundamentals of type design and its history, and they will encourage more young people into the fold. One video ('Establish Brief') suggests that it is always a good idea to do a little research before designing a new face, lest someone has got there before you. 'Let's say you think there should be a very nice italic typeface to set poetry, perhaps you might want to look it up to see if there is someone who's already done a project similar to your idea. That doesn't mean you should give up your idea, but just be aware of what other solutions people have had.' If you had given up once you realised someone had already made Snell Roundhand (Matthew Carter, 1966), then no one would have made Putteri Script (Rinaldi Novianda, 2020), Bergenia Script Font Duo (Mur Zani, 2019), Last Beyond (Risca Anitawani, 2022), Bluehill (Faja Abdul Fatah, 2019), Blackstar (Kurniadi Saputra, 2019), Audacity Script (Reza Haitami, 2020) or several hundred others.*

---

* For Lynne Yun's excellent rudiments of type design go here: typedesignschool.com

I asked Yun about the pleasure principle. The life of a young typeface designer is very much what it has always been, irrespective of the production process and consumer outlet – a combination of startling creativity and stultifying frustration. Yun's first job was at Apple, an incredible opportunity for a 21-year-old graphic designer just out of college. But she did not design an alphabet, she designed one number. For more than two months she was assigned to make the 8 that would serve as the icon for Apple's new mobile operating system iOS 8.

'They wanted it to be a mixture of Myriad and Helvetica, the two typefaces they were using at the time. It almost drove me crazy. For two months I was just drawing an 8. Just me and my computer. They wanted me to merge them and fit it on their classic squared circle "squirkle" ... they call it a Chiclet [named after the little piece of chewing gum, it is also the shape of each key on a MacBook Pro]. And then it got released, and I think it looks OK, but then it goes on Twitter. "Oh, who drew this 8? Isn't it a little off?" They were taking my 8 apart! I can see it now. The top is too thick. I didn't really know anything about optical compensation.'

A while afterwards Yun got a job at Monotype customising existing typefaces and providing creative advice to clients. She made Trade Gothic

Display and Trade Gothic Inline, two multidimensional additions to the classic sans serif face from 1948, and at weekends she worked on a freelance project called Ampersandist, a big blocky irregular design reflecting her love of calligraphy, the sort of cut-out alphabet Matisse might have made. I had first come across Yun talking about Ampersandist on the design podcast *Wireframe* in 2021, where she was asked to describe Ampersandist in terms of its personality.

'I imagine it's this hippy but still millennial-ish tech person that's living out their lives in the woods. But I really like this person. I do feel like there is this authenticness that is coming from this lifestyle.' (Yun herself divided the first eighteen years of her life between South Korea and the United States. She says her awareness of type began by spending a lot of time in public libraries and watching television with captions.)

The podcast pretended to be at a party, where all the guests were fonts: Times New Roman was polite and formal; Arial was harmless but boring; Comic Sans was annoying and played a kazoo. Another guest on the show was Emma Tucker, a writer at *Creative Review* magazine, who spoke about how, in 2019, Comic Sans had been 'weaponised' on the Conservative Party's Twitter account to promote

Brexit. 'Many mocked the choice of font,' she explained, 'but considering Comic Sans's much-derided place in the world of type, it's hard to believe the person making these graphics didn't know exactly what they were doing.'

Tucker observed that the predictable outrage surrounding its use showed 'the dark side of Comic Sans … it can play on people's hatred of it to get that message through social networks.'

Khoi Vinh, the host of the podcast, then suggested that Comic Sans was 'actually a force for evil … And yet, it endures. It's like the cockroach of typefaces!'

Lynne Yun was then asked whether there was anything she would change about the public perception of how a type was created. She said she thought it would be good for people to understand 'that they're made by real people. I think a lot of people don't realise that. I distinctly remember I was on a fishing trip, and we were going out to sea and [the skipper] was asking everyone, "What do you do, what do you do?" And I said I was a type designer and he looked at me and with a genuine look on his face and said, "I thought they were all made already, you still need to make them?"'

Dominic Girard, one of the producers of the podcast, chimed in. 'You know, Lynne, I bet that skipper on that boat trip is a Comic Sans user.'

Yun's assertion that fonts were created by humans inevitably led to the question 'But for how long?' Artificial intelligence is already imagining how its typefaces might look. In June 2023 I gave the 'human-like' chatbot ChatGPT a simple task: 'Please create an exciting typeface for me,' I tapped on my phone. It obliged within three seconds:

Certainly! I can describe a fictional exciting typeface for you. Keep in mind that I can only provide a textual description; I cannot create visual designs directly. However, you can use the description as a basis for designing the typeface or share it with a graphic designer who can bring it to life.

Name: Blaze Serif

Description: Blaze Serif is a dynamic and electrifying typeface that commands attention with its energetic and captivating design. It combines elements of both serif and display fonts, creating a unique and bold visual experience.

Letterforms: The letterforms of Blaze Serif are tall and slender, with sharp edges and distinctive,

exaggerated serifs. The vertical strokes have a
slight curve, giving the characters a sense of
forward momentum.

ChatGPT also described Blaze Serif's weight and
proportions. It had a medium-to-heavy weight,
making it suitable for 'impactful' headlines and titles. The characters had an elongated proportion,
'amplifying their intensity'. The typeface featured
some very distinct letters, including the uppercase
S, C and Q, 'which add an element of unpredict-
ability', and various lowercase letters which have
'unexpected angles or loops, creating a sense of
movement and excitement.'

And then we came to the 'texture' of the face,
which was the detail a viewer might notice first, and
which a human designer might have intended from
the start. 'Blaze Serif incorporates a subtle texture
that mimics the appearance of glowing embers …
The edges of the characters are slightly irregular, as
if they were forged in a blazing fire. The serifs themselves are pointed, resembling fiery sparks bursting
from the ends of the strokes.'

I found this both exciting and disturbing. I worried for Lynne Yun's future, and I worried for mine.
ChatGPT's description of Blaze Serif (which is an
original name, although several other Blazes exist)

was unnervingly close to how I and other writers on type might depict such a fiery alphabet, which shouldn't be surprising, as this is where the chatbot has obtained its descriptive prowess. More disturbing still was the likelihood that within a few years this description would appear onscreen as the type itself.

A day later I asked ChatGPT to create me another typeface. 'Certainly!' it replied. But this time it wanted to know about my intended use, including 'the desired tone or personality (e.g., playful, elegant, futuristic).'

'Certainly!' I answered. 'Something to put on a book jacket and perhaps a cereal packet.'

> Great! Based on your input, I'll create a versatile typeface that can work well on both book jackets and cereal packets. Here's a description of the typeface:
>
> Name: Adventura
>
> Style: Adventura is a dynamic and energetic typeface that combines elements of playfulness and sophistication. It exudes a sense of adventure, making it suitable for various applications, from captivating book covers to eye-catching cereal packaging.

This time, ChatGPT reminded me of my eleven-year-old self answering an exam question. I gave it a B+ for a good effort. Adventura's element of 'playfulness' made me think of Comic Sans.

> Thank you for your feedback. I'm glad you found my response to be a good effort. I apologize if my description of Adventura gave the impression that it is similar to Comic Sans. That was not my intention. It is a unique typeface … I would be happy to modify the description or provide further assistance.

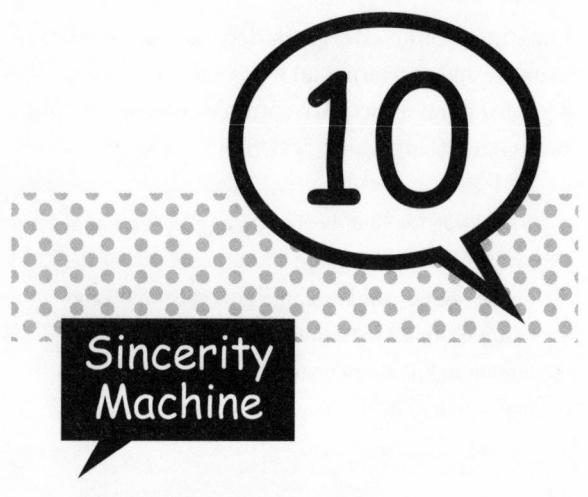

Sincerity Machine

If AI typefaces were the future, would all the irony be lost in the past? In 2014 the artist Jesse England, working in Pittsburgh, Pennsylvania, made something he called his Sincerity Machine, a manual Brother typewriter on which he had changed each of the standard keys to Comic Sans. He had recently begun working with laser engraving machines, which he found made very precise rubber stamps, and he had glued tiny green Comic Sans characters onto the existing ones. 'A typewriter is a kind of stamping tool,' he told me, 'and I subconsciously combined technical possibilities and some ideas about performing authenticity.'

He referred to his project as 'benign audacity', and the response on social media and from international art news outlets was 'massive and immediate', the most publicised project he'd made. His other work had also combined old and new technologies in incongruous ways (such as photocopying pages from a book on a Kindle), but the addition of Comic Sans – as it tended to do – ignited the interest far beyond what he would have achieved had he replaced the typewriter keys with Futura or Cooper Black.

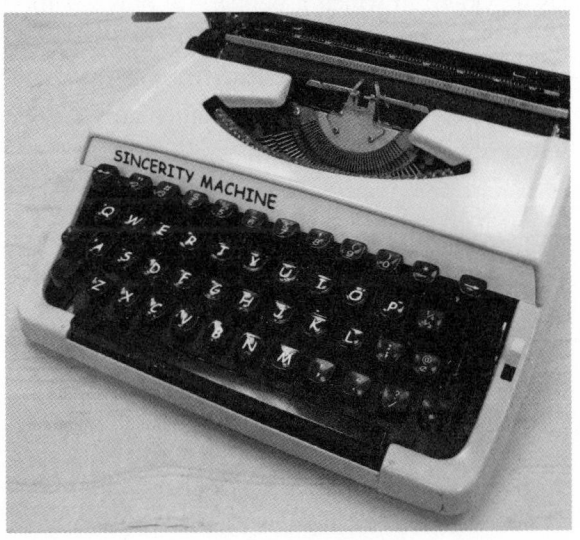

A comic type: Jesse England questions authority and authenticity.

'Comic Sans occupies a peculiar spot in graphic design because it usually signifies one of two things,' England reasoned. 'The user's naiveté in not knowing it is a "bad" font, or the user's tongue-in-cheek usage of it as a joke. For the former, it is a revealing mark of sincerity for this "detested" font to be presented in a professional setting.' The manual typewriter had itself become a superficial but reliable symbol of purity, but his new conflation made one question this.

One of England's other projects involved a series of videos in which a person (we only see their hands) learns to 'draw' famous types by hand. The choices include Helvetica, Papyrus, Jokerman and Comic Sans, and a video of the latter carries a deft but eerily detached commentary:

> We'll start by tracing the letters to help break
> away from your previous handwriting influence …
> While it aims to look like handwriting, Comic Sans
> exists in some impossible realm between machine
> and human creation. That's why it's important to
> pay extra close attention to the longer uncurled
> section called 'stems', because they're always
> bending ever so slightly in strange places and at
> seemingly random angles. While handwriting this
> font, one is always acting against common sense …

but … Comic Sans is surely the most sincere font
in popular use.

There was a link to download and print a practice
sheet, and the examples to trace used the typeface to
its full potential:

Birthday party for Chris at 10.15 in

the 2nd Floor break room!!!

Garage Sale this Saturday

in Evergreen Court! 7AM,

NO EARLIES.

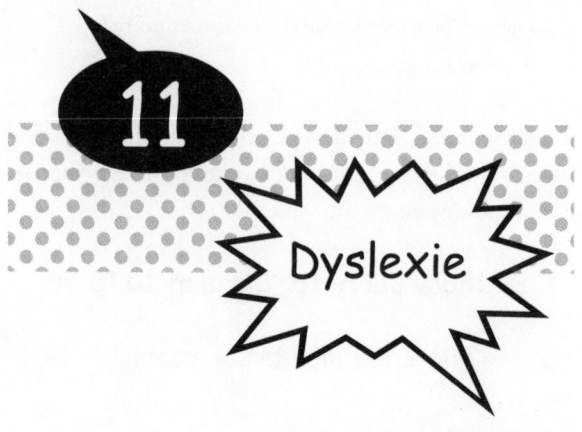

In early 2023, the British Dyslexia Association (BDA) updated its style guide. It was a clear, simple and very old-fashioned looking document, loaded with bullet points on how educators, printers and designers might facilitate ease of reading. It explained that it was always good to give text plenty of space with lots of subheadings and other structural tools to help readers navigate. Use less white paper and more cream or soft pastel colours, matt rather than gloss, and increase contrast levels between text and background. When it came to fonts, the plainer sans serifs were best, with lots of spacing (inter-word spacing should be at least 3.5 times the inter-letter spacing). Arial or Comic Sans were ideal; Verdana, Tahoma and Trebuchet were also good.

Comic Sans found its value in classrooms long before academics or professional associations began to recommend it as a tool, but the two weren't entirely unconnected. Few dispute the old maxim that 'we read best what we read most'; familiarity eases us swiftly from an awareness of the type to an awareness of the text – content over presentation. A child's awareness of letterforms seen early and often – Comic Sans, of course, but also friendly faces such as Verdana and Arial Rounded MT Bold – will embed a sense of comprehension that will later be challenged by 'tougher' serifs such as Times New Roman or Caslon. Most readers will make that transition with time; those with reading difficulties may take longer, or rely on familiar, rounder shapes to assist them.

Other design factors may also assist a reader, not least the lack of ambiguity between lower-case b and d (and p and q), and wide and open inner counters to ensure sufficient space between letters. In the last twenty years several fonts with these attributes have been developed specifically to help those with reading difficulties, among them Dyslexie and OpenDyslexic, and their creators have made fluent claims. But in a survey of the literature up to 2014 (a review of more than thirty studies), the type designer Charles Bigelow found that there was insufficient evidence to recommend anything in particular. Bigelow and his partner Kris Holmes had created the popular Lucida type family in 1985 and had spent many years considering the questions of legibility and readability. But they reasoned that typefaces were only a part of the problem, as all the other basic questions of typography – layout, spacing, point size, line length and contrast – also played a crucial part. The enquiries into dyslexia also suggested that the personal taste of the reader was always going to be another consideration: 'suitable' fonts are always going to be in competition with favourite fonts, as the story of Comic Sans has always made clear.*

Some people *do* dispute the old maxim that 'we read best what we read most', at least when it comes to comprehension. Small-scale studies have shown that, faced with factual information in both easy-to-read and more consciously elaborate typefaces, the latter process, known as disfluency,

---

* And the personal experiences of those with dyslexia speak loudest of all. 'The day my sister, Jessica, discovered Comic Sans, her entire world changed,' the journalist Lauren Hudgins wrote in the online magazine The Establishment in 2019. Jessica told her that 'being able to use Comic Sans is similar to a mobility aid, or a visual aid, or a hearing aid,' and it was a key factor in enabling her to complete her university course. While acknowledging the humorous elements of Ban Comic Sans and Comic Sans Criminal, she finds them 'quite elitist' and 'belittling and condescending'.

requires deeper concentration and may increase memory retention.

In 2010 a small study at Princeton University presented a group of students with a story about extraterrestrials in both easy and challenging fonts. According to the university's own report, the students were given ninety seconds to memorise information about the aliens, were then distracted for fifteen minutes, and then tested. Those who read about the aliens in 16-point Arial Pure Black answered correctly 72.8 per cent of the time, compared to 86.5 per cent of those who read about them in 12-point Comic Sans MS or Bodoni MT.

The second experiment expanded the sample from 28 university students to 222 high school pupils. Now the hard-to-read fonts were Haettenschweiler, Monotype Corsiva and Comic Sans Italicized. The control type was usually Times New Roman or Arial.

The findings were similar, although the size of the type may again have had an impact. The researchers were upbeat, suggesting they have uncovered 'a no-cost policy fix that could really improve students' learning. While we do need to further test the theory, if we are right, schools across the country could potentially see significant results without making a dent in school budgets.'

But this thinking is at least a century old. In 1917 the Russian literary theorist Viktor Shklovsky wrote how one purpose of art is to shake us from a stupor, to help us 'recover the sensation of life; it exists to make one feel things; to make the stone stony'. By making the most familiar objects unfamiliar, perception might be heightened. This might also serve as an adequate explanation for why so many were both attracted to and outraged by Comic Sans.

What if one could consciously control this memory retention process with a custom-made font designed specifically for this purpose? In

2018, researchers at the Royal Melbourne Institute of Technology conducted an experiment using Arial and a newly developed typeface called Sans Forgetica (not an April fool: Sans Forgetica was backward-slanting and had gaps in each letter to reduce reading speed). Among four hundred students, 57 per cent of text in Sans Forgetica was remembered well, compared to 50 per cent in Arial.

But two years later, the journal *Memory* reported that further research involving a student sample twice the size found that use of the new font aided neither learning nor memory, and in some cases actually impaired recall. The conclusion was damning – 'our findings suggest that Sans Forgetica really is forgettable' – but also open-ended. The fact that no one type consistently helped with even short-term fact retention pointed to just one thing: we still needed a large range of types to suit different people and fulfil different needs. In a phrase that would only cheer type designers the world over, it was back to the drawing board.

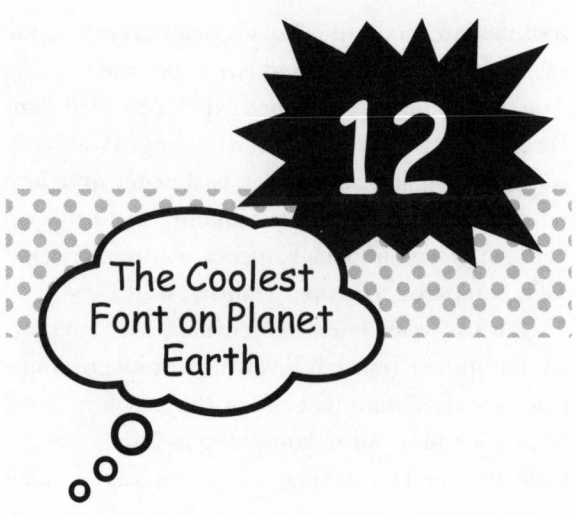

12

The Coolest
Font on Planet
Earth

Then Dave and Holly Combs changed their minds. Or at least Dave did. One day in 2019, one half of the couple responsible for the Ban Comic Sans campaign decided to amend the message to Use Comic Sans. Dave had decided he didn't want 'anyone to be mean to anyone' any more. His wife didn't agree: 'He's too nice,' she said. She still believed the font shouldn't be so widely employed.

*
*
*

Vincent Connare says he has only used Comic Sans once in anger. 'I was having trouble changing my broadband to Sky, so wrote them a letter in Comic Sans, saying how disappointed I was. I got a £10 refund. In those cases, I would recommend it.'

Connare's letter made the news, as most interesting or novel uses of Comic Sans tended to do. In 2013, the retirement of Pope Benedict XVI was marked with the online publication of a 62-page digital photo album commemorating his travels. Captions in Comic Sans. Twitter storm. When the basketball star LeBron James wore a T-shirt with the Black Lives Matter slogan 'I Can't Breathe' in 2014, the controversy concerned his protest rather than the choice of Comic Sans as the typeface. In 2019, John Dowd, a former lawyer for Donald Trump, issued a letter in Comic Sans explaining why potentially incriminating documents involving Rudy Giuliani would not be released. Again, Twitter storm. In 2022, a viewer of Disney+ discovered they had the option of watching a programme with captions in Comic Sans. Storm.

But it was nothing like what happened when *The Face* did something extraordinary with Comic Sans for its print issue in March 2023.

For those who didn't wait by the kiosk at the end of Kingsway in London for the van drop of each new monthly issue of *The Face* in 1980 and 1981 (as I did!), the magazine may not mean so much. *The Face* was a revolution, as much as *Cosmopolitan*, *Rolling Stone* or the Sunday colour supplements had been in the 1960s. It took the elements of a good music magazine and added layers of fashion, club culture and other cool young arts. Above all it looked extraordinary, the work of its daring young designer Neville Brody. Text and photos bled in all directions as desktop publishing found its purpose and energy. New Romantics, Britpop and Madchester all found their natural home in its pages, and while the internet determined its inevitable decline, its fortunes were recently revived with digital online stories and thick quarterly print editions.

The Spring 2023 edition featured more than three hundred pages. It opened with the big-money adverts – Ferragamo, Guess, Gucci, Prada, Moschino. It progressed to Fake Showbiz News ('HBO announces season three of *The White Lotus* will be set in Margate'), and then to a vox pop of middle-aged men who may decide the outcome of the next election ('What are the issues you care about most? Fuel poverty, the energy crisis, the NHS'), and then a look at Greta Gerwig's Barbie movie. There was a big interview with musician/actor Halle Bailey, a lot of fashion spreads, a story about the rapper RXK

Nephew, more fashion spreads involving an Alsatian
and a pregnant woman, a profile of the actor Ewan
Mitchell, a feature about female delivery drivers, and
a celebration of the work of Vivienne Westwood. All

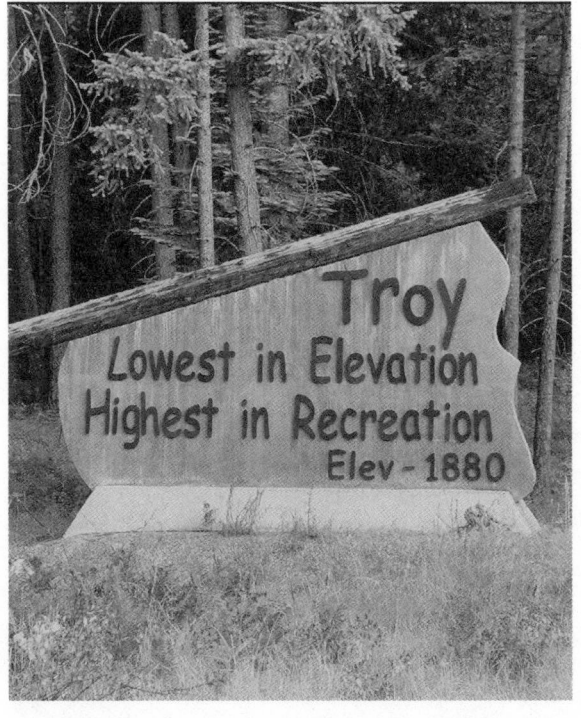

Up for fun: The tiny town of Troy raises the bar in Montana.

the text, from the magazine's name to the back-page interview with a 74-year-old photographer and carp angler, was in Comic Sans. There was nothing else. And all the Comic Sans text was treated with a swirl of rainbow colours, which presented even more of a challenge. As the magazine explained on its website, 'Comic Sans always elicits a strong reaction. Whether that's excitement or discomfort, we'll leave up to you. Feeling positive about Comic Sans could be seen as bad taste, while feeling negative about it could be interpreted as snobbery ... What matters most is that it isn't boring and can stand the test of time. Our least favourite typefaces are ones that provoke zero reactions.'

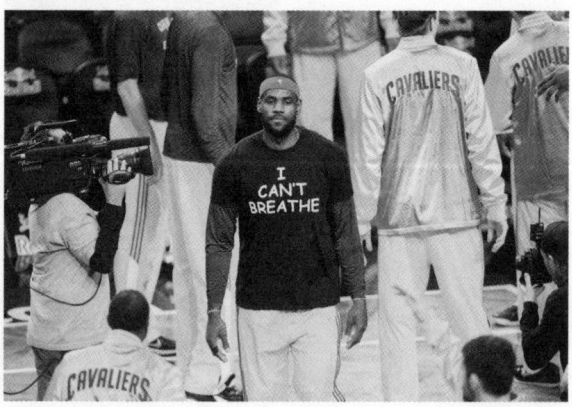

A common language: LeBron James makes his voice heard.

But it wasn't quite Comic Sans. It was another revision, this one created by the graphic design studio Eurostandard and called ComicFace. The round letters were a little fatter, the stems a little straighter, and the monospacing made it a little easier on the eye when spread over an entire page. It still looked odd, arresting. The designers reported that their new version initially looked a little too linear, so they enlisted a friend's seven-year-old child to inject a sense of spontaneity.

What was most remarkable about the magazine was how little commotion it caused on publication. No storm. It quickly sold out its print run, but beyond a few raised eyebrows on TikTok, the comments on social media were about subject, not form, about Halle Bailey and Vivienne Westwood, which is how things usually are with content.

What did that mean for the typeface? It was ironic. It was post-ironic. Nobody knew. Nobody really seemed to care much either. Comic Sans was now just *there*, like something standard, something permanent. Which meant that after thirty years of trouble, everyone could now go back to what they were doing just before it was made.

Bibliography, References and Further Reading

I would like to thank everyone who helped me with this book, especially Vincent Connare and Toshi Omagari for their expertise and provision of illustrations.

This is the first book about Comic Sans. Or rather, this is the first book specifically about the history of Comic Sans the typeface. Unlike other typefaces, Comic Sans has inspired many titles which use it as a punchline or an accessory, including (but not limited to) The Holy Bible printed in Comic Sans; Comic Sans Murder; Comic Sans for the Ex: Thistlewood Star Mysteries #5; and El Misterio de la Comic Sans.

Thankfully there are also a few good books which examine the development and design of type in general and digital type in particular, and I'm happy to recommend a selection here. The list is followed by a few of the most interesting discussions of Comic Sans online.

Anderson, Gail and Heller, Stephen, *The Typography Idea Book* (London: Laurence King, 2012)

Coles, Stephen, *The Anatomy of Type: A Graphic Guide to 100 Typefaces* (New York: Harper Design, 2012)

De Jong, Cees W.; Purvis, Alkston W.; Tholenaar, Jan, *Type: A Visual History of Typefaces* (Cologne: Taschen, 2022)

Henestrosa, Cristóbal; Mesegeur, Laura; Scaglione, José, *How To Create Typefaces* (Madrid: Tipo E Editorial, 2012)

Hyndman, Sarah, *Why Fonts Matter* (London: Virgin Books, 2016)

Lupton, Ellen, *Thinking with Type* (Princeton Architectural Press, 2010)

McNeil, Paul, *The Visual History of Type* (London: Laurence King, 2017)

Sagmeister, Stefan, *Things I Have Learned in My Life So Far* (New York: Abrams, 2013)

Samara, Timothy, *Letterforms: Typeface Design from Past to Future* (Beverly, MA: Rockport, 2018)

White, Alex W., *Thinking in Type* (New York: Allworth Press, 2005)

Preface: The ABC of Fonts

Incunabula Short Title Catalogue at the British Library: **data.cerl.org/istc**

Andrew Solomon's op-ed: **nytimes.com/2004/07/10/opinion/the-closingof-the-american-book.html**

1. Fabiola

CERN's big breakthrough, the full video: **youtube.com/watch?v=AzXodwbY4Yk**

And the reaction: **theverge.com/2012/7/4/3136652/cern-scientists-comic-sans-higgs-boson**

2. You Don't Clown Around with a Clown

The April Fool: **home.cern/news/news/cern/cern-switch-comic-sans**

Google's attempt: **huffpost.com/entry/google-helvetica-comic-sansapril-fools-2011_n_843586**

3. Copa del Rey

The Athletic's full *Football Clichés* podcast:
theathletic.com/podcast/
164-football-cliches/?episode=196

4. Vincent

Vincent Connare's website: **connare.com**

5. Melinda Gates Now Takes Full Responsibility

A walk-through of Microsoft Bob with some great images: **toastytech.com/guis/bob.html**
   Melinda Gates offers career advice: **youtube. com/watch?v=dtE-1wylglA**
   And a fuller explanation here: **linkedin.com/ pulse/failure-taughtme-lesson-ill-never- forget-melindagates/?linkId=4324408**

6. Holly and Dave

A film of the Combs explaining their distaste, and some merchandise opportunities: **linktr.ee/ bancomicsans**

In praise of Comic Sans: **theguardian. com/commentisfree/2009/apr/28/ leader-praise-comic-sans-typography**
You may still send someone an admonishing email from here: **comicsanscriminal.com**

7. The Most Interesting Person I've Met

The exciting work of Bruno Maag can be sampled here: **daltonmaag.com**

8. Chick Chack, Autumnilla, Memorita

The work of Abdul Malik Wisnu and hundreds of others is here: **myfonts.com**

But this too is a perilous rabbit hole for anyone who is likely to end up spending hours reading about fonts: **fontshop.com**

To see if *Print* magazine's 2016 Best New Typefaces of the Year still appeal, check them out here: **printmag.com/design-culture/ the-best-new-typefaces-of-2016-so-far-anyway**

More thoughts from Toshi Omagari on his Comic Code: **tosche.net/fonts/comic-code**

More on the National Board on Printing Type Faces, including a longer extract from the minutes: **paulshawletterdesign.com/2014/06/stop-making-type-the-quixiotic-quest-of-the-national-board-on-printing-type-faces/**

9. Too Many Types?

Jan Tschichold's manifesto (and other things) under discussion here: **designhistory.org/Avant_Garde_pages/DieNeueType.html**

And here: **studiointernational.com/jan-tschichold-andthe-new-typography-review-bard-graduatecenter-gallery**

Lynne Yun's fine portfolio is here: **lynneyun.com**

10. Sincerity Machine

Jesse England's Sincerity Machine and his other disruptions are here: **jesseengland.net/project/ sincerity-machine-the-comicsans-typewriter**

And his typeface videos are here: **youtube. com/watch?v=R5a2hapPVMk**

11. Dyslexie

The claims for Dyslexie are here: **dyslexiefont.com**

The Princeton disfluency project is here: **princeton.edu/news/2010/10/28/ font-focus-making-ideas-harder-read- maymake-them-easier-retain**

The Sans Forgetica study is here: **rmit.edu.au/news/all-news/2018/oct/ sans-forgetica-news-story**

Highly recommended survey of the research around disfluency: **cognitiveresearchjournal. springeropen.com/articles/10.1186/ s41235-022-00448-**

12. The Coolest Font on Planet Earth

The Face explains its choice: **theface.com/culture/
eurostandard-interview-graphicdesign-
typography-comic-sans-font**

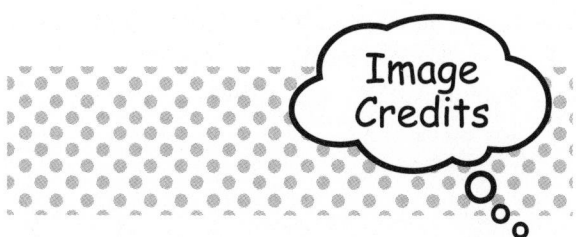

Image Credits

105 'Up for fun' (Spend A Day Touring, LLC, CC BY-SA 2.0, via Wikimedia Commons)
106 'A common language' (Rich Kane Photography / Alamy Stock Photo)

Index